An Introduction to Democracy

T0097313

AN INTRODUCTION TO DEMOCRACY

EAMONN BUTLER

Institute of
Economic Affairs

First published in Great Britain in 2021 by
The Institute of Economic Affairs
2 Lord North Street
Westminster
London SW1P 3LB
in association with London Publishing Partnership Ltd
www.londonpublishingpartnership.co.uk

The mission of the Institute of Economic Affairs is to improve understanding of the fundamental institutions of a free society by analysing and expounding the role of markets in solving economic and social problems.

A CIP catalogue record for this book is available from the British Library.

ISBN 978-0-255-36797-4

Many IEA publications are translated into languages other than English or are reprinted. Permission to translate or to reprint should be sought from the Director General at the address above.

Typeset in Kepler by T&T Productions Ltd
www.tandtproductions.com

Printed and bound by CPI Group (UK) Ltd, Croydon, CR0 4YY

CONTENTS

ABOUT THE AUTHOR

Eamonn Butler is Director of the Adam Smith Institute, one of the world's leading policy think tanks. He holds degrees in economics and psychology, a PhD in philosophy, and an honorary DLitt. In the 1970s he worked in Washington for the US House of Representatives, and taught philosophy at Hillsdale College, Michigan, before returning to the UK to help found the Adam Smith Institute. A former winner of the Freedom Medal awarded by Freedoms Foundation of Valley Forge and the UK National Free Enterprise Award, Eamonn is currently Secretary of the Mont Pelerin Society.

Eamonn is the author of many books, including introductions to the pioneering economists and thinkers Adam Smith, Milton Friedman, F. A. Hayek, Ludwig von Mises and Ayn Rand. He has also published primers on classical liberalism, public choice, Magna Carta and the Austrian School of Economics, as well as *The Condensed Wealth of Nations, The Best Book on the Market, School of Thought: 101 Great Liberal Thinkers* and *An Introduction to Entrepreneurship*. His *Foundations of a Free Society* won the 2014 Fisher Prize. He is co-author of *Forty Centuries of Wage and Price Controls*, and of a series of books on IQ. He is a frequent contributor to print, broadcast and online media.

1 UNDERSTANDING DEMOCRACY

What this book is about

This book is a straightforward introduction to democracy: what it is and how it works, its strengths and weaknesses, its benefits and its limitations. The main aim of the book is to enable *anyone* to understand democracy, even if they have never experienced it. But many who *think* they understand democracy should benefit too, because even they often overlook its most critical features.

Understanding democracy is important: after all, two-thirds of the world's population, in over a hundred countries, live under governments that claim to be democratic. And since very few of those governments actually live up to the ideals of democracy or respect its key principles and institutions, a *clear* understanding of democracy is even more important. In particular, we should be aware of how easily democracy can be lost or abused when people do not properly understand it.

To achieve these aims, the book defines democracy, explains its purposes, and shows the difference between genuine democracy and the many sham versions that currently exist. It outlines the history of democracy, the changing nature of the idea and the different ways of achieving it. It summarises the benefits of democracy but also the many myths about it that blind us to its limitations. Lastly, the book asks why people have become so disillusioned with democratic politics today – and what if anything can be done about it.

The problem of 'democracy'

The biggest problem for anyone trying to understand democracy is that the word has changed its meaning. What we call 'democracy' today is not what the ancient Greeks (who are credited with inventing the idea) had in mind. To them 'democracy' meant a system of government in which the citizens would gather in open assemblies to make laws, decide key policies (such as whether to go to war), and appoint officials. To us, however, 'democracy' means a system of government in which the public vote, every few years, to elect representatives (such as presidents, members of parliament or senators) who then decide on laws, policies and public appointments.

But even this modern usage can cover many different meanings. The word 'democracy' may describe systems in which elections are free and fair, with secret ballots and a range of candidates to choose from, and where there are limits on the powers of representatives and officials, with an independent court system to ensure that they act legally and within those limits. On the other hand, 'democracy' is often used to describe systems in which some of those features are less than ideal or even missing. In many countries that call themselves 'democratic', ballots are not truly secret, election officials act dishonestly, voters and candidates are intimidated, the media control the public debate, and representatives are corrupt.

In some cases, countries display the trappings of democracy (such as elections, parliaments and courts) but only one party is allowed to field candidates. Policymakers and judges never question the authority of the ruler, and officials have almost unlimited powers over the lives and conduct of citizens. An example is North Korea, where turnout at elections is nearly 100 per cent and the share of the vote given to candidates from the Democratic Front for the Reunification of the Fatherland is nearly unanimous (which rings loud alarm bells).

Limiting democracy

A common misconception about democracy is that it gives the majority the right to do what it wants. But a little thought shows that this is plainly mistaken. How can mere election success give a majority party the right to confiscate the minority's homes, businesses and wealth, for example? Or to imprison or deport them, torture them or even slaughter them? Human beings have values that are higher than majority rule – such as the sanctity of people's lives, freedom and property. The fact that a majority decides to violate those values does not make their action morally or politically right.

Some 2,400 years ago, Ancient Greek thinkers such as Plato and his pupil Aristotle understood this. Indeed, they regarded democracy as a very dangerous form of government, and not just because they were wealthy aristocrats. Democracy could too easily become rule by the mob, under which no person's life or possessions would be safe. 'Where justice is not sovereign', wrote Aristotle (350 BC) in his *Politics*, 'the people become a monarch' and 'aim at sole power and become like a master'.

Two millennia later, the 55 landowners, slaveholders and other prominent individuals who drew up the Constitution of the new United States of America had similar concerns. They created, not a Greek-style *democracy* in which everything would be decided by the people, but a democratic *republic* in which the people would elect representatives to take decisions on their behalf. They carefully designed the decision-making process to limit the power of those in office specifically to protect individuals and minorities – though shamefully they did not extend these protections to the quarter of the population who were slaves or Native Americans.

The need for democratic institutions to serve our values rather than dictate our lives is why the most genuine form of democracy (in the modern meaning), and the one which captures the real spirit of the democratic idea, is what is called *liberal democracy*. Those who advocate it believe that the core purpose of democracy is not to restrict or control people but to liberate them. To these *liberals* (in the European sense), government is not created to force individuals to do whatever the majority decide is 'right', but to keep everyone as free as possible and to minimise the use of force and coercion – either by other people or the state (Butler 2015a).

But that peace and freedom require that majority rule must be limited. In a genuinely liberal democracy, say liberals, not even an overwhelming majority – a thousand to one, say – can do as they please: the majority must always respect and uphold the basic rights and freedoms of all individuals. Those rights and freedoms take priority over the majority view because the reason why government exists is to protect them.

Liberals agree less on precisely what the rights of individuals actually are, and where they come from. Nevertheless, individual rights seem to be more extensive and better protected in relatively liberal democracies than elsewhere. That, argues the American political economist Jayme Lemke (2016), may be due to competition between different political systems, inducing people to migrate to freer jurisdictions that respect the individuality of their citizens.

The attraction of democracy

Those who support democracy argue that laws should not be made on the whim of some elite individual (such as a king or a dictator) or group (such as a ruling family or aristocracy). Instead, the *general public* should decide what laws they live under – or, at least, should choose who makes the laws. These choices, they insist, should be made on the basis of political equality, where everyone's vote counts equally. Ideally, as many citizens as possible should be allowed to vote. People should be free to think and speak out on issues of importance. Ideally, electors should be well informed, competent and rational about their own governance. And there should be stable, trusted and honest institutions that fairly translate the public's decisions into policy.

These democratic ideals seem powerfully attractive. After all, who would *not* like a say in how they are governed, rather than have someone else decide events for them? Who would *not* like to be spared the brute force of dictators? Who would *not* like to think that their opinion counts, and is counted fairly?

Indeed, these democratic ideals are so widely attractive that, unfortunately, almost all governments claim to cherish them, whether they do or not. Being called 'democratic' is a mark of respect and approval. As the twentieth-century English novelist and critic George Orwell (1946) noted: 'It is almost universally felt that when we call a country democratic we are praising it; consequently, the defenders of every kind of regime claim that it is a democracy'.

The result is that the word 'democracy' then loses its meaning. Majority parties regard victory in 'democratic' elections as giving them full authority to persecute others, raid public funds for their own benefit, and give out government jobs and contracts to their cronies. Dictators jail their political opponents and stage sham elections that deliver them 100 per cent of the vote and then claim to be 'democratically elected'. In many places, merely criticising government leaders and their policies can get you arrested for treason. Abuses like these are offensive to the very idea of democracy.

More problems of understanding

As well as such deliberate and cynical distortions of the word's meaning, there are also genuine and widespread misunderstandings about what democracy really is and how it works. Many people in Asia, for example, reject democracy as producing conflict, indecision and short-termism. They overlook its strength, popularity and resilience. Many Westerners, by contrast, believe that democracy is the sole key to prosperity, freedom, equality and peace. Their view of democracy is so rosy that they fail to see its problems and limitations.

Indeed, the adulation of democracy is perhaps the biggest threat to it. Its enthusiasts often claim democracy as the best system of government because it rests on the approval of the majority. But if majority voting is really the best way to make decisions, why should we not use it for every decision? The argument persuades many that we should; but the sad result is that everyday decisions that were once left to individuals – how they live, what they eat or drink, even what they might say in public – are becoming increasingly subject to what majority opinion will allow.

According to liberals, this burdens democracy with a task that it is not designed for. Democracy, they say, was never intended to do any more than make the few collective decisions that people could not make individually – such as mutual defence. It was developed to safeguard individuals' rights, not to curtail them at the whim of the majority. It was meant to expand people's freedoms, not to shrink them. It was created to minimise coercion over people, not to legitimise it.

The need for clarity

In worshipping the benefits of democracy, it is easy to lose sight of its limits. Majority decision-making is not the answer to every problem. It is merely a plausible method of taking the (comparatively few) decisions that can only be made collectively. Liberals argue that democracy is not a means to subvert or supplant the (very many) decisions that individuals can make perfectly well themselves, and that it works only where that freedom is respected.

There is also a huge gap between the ideal of democracy and the flawed reality of the political process through which it works. When majority decision-making is over-expanded, then politics – being an inevitable part of collective decision-making – creeps into every aspect of life, large and small, polluting the very idea of democracy. The danger then is that people become hostile to 'democracy', thinking it solely about the power of political interests – and that we abandon the very system that might protect us from just that.

This is why it is so important to be clear about what democracy is – and is not. We need to be able to identify which of the many political systems that claim to be 'democratic' actually live up to democracy's ideals and principles. To understand democracy's core purpose and recognise its limitations. To learn which questions democracy is fit to decide and which it is not. To discover what promotes good democratic government and what corrupts it. To accept that there are higher values that we must defend, even from an overwhelming majority of opinion. To realise that democracy must be kept within its limits. To appreciate that democracy rests on moral, cultural and institutional foundations that need to be maintained and are hard to reproduce. And to remain aware that democracy requires considerable effort to understand, operate and preserve.

2 THE HISTORY OF DEMOCRACY

The word 'democracy' came into English from six-teenth-century France, but its origins are much older. Around 4,000–5,000 years ago, the Mycenaean-era Greeks referred to population groups as *damos*, though the term might have come from *dumu*, a similar concept of the even older Sumerian civilisation in what is now southern Iraq. In Classical Greek this became *demos*, which could mean 'people' or the 'mass' of poorer residents. Together with *kratos*, meaning 'power' or 'control', it provides the root of the modern word.

Greek democracy

The Sumerians who settled in Mesopotamia – the 'fertile crescent' between the Tigris and Euphrates rivers – around 5,000 years ago are credited with founding the world's first known civilisation. Some scholars contend that they may even have had an early form of democracy, and that the kings of their city states, like Gilgamesh of Uruk, did not hold total power but functioned within councils of elders. However, the evidence is very thin.

Even further east, some version of democracy may have emerged among the independent 'republics' of the Indian subcontinent around 2,600 years ago. Once again, their monarchs, the Rajas, ruled within deliberative assemblies, which were open to all free men, had wide political authority and met regularly. But little detail exists, and scholars are similarly divided on whether such arrangements were truly examples of popular power.

There is, however, plenty of evidence that democracy peaked in Greece (notably Athens) around 2,500 years ago. In fact, there were around 1,000 small democracies in Classical Greece: each was an independent city-state (the *polis* from which the word 'politics' comes). In such small communities, however, power can easily accumulate in the hands of an elite few. The idea of democracy was to prevent this and to have policy decided by a wider group. It was still only a minority of the population, since even in 'democratic' Athens, slaves, children, women and foreigners were all excluded. Even so, some 6,000–10,000 Athenian men, gathering at open meetings, would debate and decide on matters such as laws, wars and the appointment of officials.

The democratic ideal was famously articulated by the Athenian statesman and general Pericles (*c.* 431 BC): collective sovereignty, political equality, freedom and toleration, and respect for the law, for others and for one's own duties. But the power and fickleness of popular assemblies alarmed ancient thinkers such as Plato and Aristotle. They believed the mass of poorer citizens were too ill-informed and short-sighted to know their own best interests and could be easily swayed by demagogues. They worried that popular democracy might turn into a new form of tyranny – rule by the mob. And they feared that the mob would simply rob better-off people (like themselves), claiming that a majority vote made such robbery just and legitimate.

Plato's solution was to leave governing to wise 'philosopher kings', but Aristotle realised that such paragons did not exist. He thought that democracy (which in Ancient Greece was effectively rule by the poor) might save citizens from *oligarchy* (effectively, rule by the rich) but that democracy in turn needed to be restrained by citizens of middling wealth – of whom there were too few.

The Roman Republic

Thinkers in ancient Rome had similar misgivings about democracy; but at least their version was restrained by an institutional framework. Though later it would be replaced by the dictatorship of the Caesars, Rome was a *republic* (from the Latin *res publica* or 'thing of the people').

A republic is a system of government that runs according to a set of rules which specify how it operates and the limits to what it can decide. These rules – sometimes written out explicitly in a *constitution* – are there to restrain the power of those in authority and protect minorities and individuals from arbitrary decisions. A republic can be 'democratic' (with the general public getting to appoint legislators to represent them) or it can be 'oligarchic' (run by a self-selecting elite); but both remain limited by the accepted rules.

The Roman Republic had some democratic and some oligarchic features. It was never really a 'thing of the people'. Its two *consuls* had near-monarchic power and were elected, not by the people, but by a committee of aristocrats. The Senate too was an aristocratic body, not elected by the public. But the eligible voters – male *cives* (citizens) – could choose (and, crucially, remove) some other important officials such as the *tribunes*, who could veto legislation, and the *magistrates* who enforced it.

Popular involvement was even more limited in times of emergency, when the Senate and consuls could appoint *dictators* – individuals given total but temporary governing authority. It was not long before the dictators turned into emperors, holding power for life. And while the first emperors were keen to retain the institutional trappings of the old Republic, there was no doubt about where power really lay.

The medieval period

Iceland's *Althing*, established around 930 and still in existence, claims to be the world's oldest parliament. It was open to all free men, who met annually before the 'Law Rock' at Thingvellir. One person, the Lawspeaker, would recite the existing laws (which suggests that there were mercifully few) and there was general debate. Yet only fifty prominent citizens actually *decided* on the laws.

In 1215, England's tyrannical King John was confronted by his nobles, who demanded he accept *Magna Carta* – a 'great charter' that limited the king's powers and in particular required the barons' assent to new laws and taxes. That became the foundation upon which England's parliament would be built (Butler 2015b).

Elsewhere in Europe around the same time, trading and commercial cities had begun to emerge, each making their own rules. This posed a challenge to the supposedly God-given authority of monarchs; but the idea grew that decisions should be made by local popular consensus and not by an all-powerful central ruler.

By the late 1400s, the Italian city-states could reasonably be called *republics*. More accurately, they were *constitutional oligarchies*: while governance centred around small groups rather than the whole public, decision-making was still subject to accepted rules. And the importance of public opinion on the political process was well recognised: in his influential work on statecraft, the diplomat and philosopher Niccolò Machiavelli (1513) advised the ruling oligarchs that their states would be much stronger if they carried the people with them.

The early modern period

In northern Europe, particularly in liberal trading economies such as the Netherlands, political power became less centralised too. The rise of democratic ideas was further helped by the Reformation of the 1500s and 1600s, stressing equality before God and promoting education and literacy: good Protestants needed to be able to read the Word of God for themselves, rather than relying on the authority of the clergy.

In the British Isles, the struggle between all-powerful (*autocratic*) monarchs and democratic ideas turned into outright civil war in the 1640s, when King Charles I tried to raise taxes without the consent of Parliament. In 1647, the Levellers, who opposed all aristocratic privilege, debated what should replace it. They called for a surprisingly modern set of institutions: a democratic government, with universal (albeit only male) suffrage, frequent elections and fair electoral boundaries, equal treatment before the law, religious tolerance, and no forced conscription. But on reaching power after deposing Charles, the Parliamentarian leader Oliver Cromwell proved no less autocratic than the monarch he replaced: he had the Levellers arrested and imposed twelve years of military rule.

This turmoil prompted much thinking on the origins and purpose of government power. The seventeenth-century English philosopher Thomas Hobbes (1651) suggested that government came out of a 'social contract' that individuals formed in order to spare them from mutual aggression and greed. He believed that a sovereign, as the 'head' of this new order, should have control, just as the head of a body does. There was no right to rebel, since any challenge to authority might return society to a condition of war. However, a subsequent English philosopher, John Locke (1689) used the same 'social contract' idea to come up with a quite different approach. He envisaged individuals setting up a state apparatus specifically to protect their individual rights and expand their freedoms. Therefore, the only power that the state had over them was merely the power that individuals had voluntarily transferred to it in order to protect themselves. Kings existed to serve the people: they could not do whatever they thought fit. And the people had the right to overthrow a monarch who betrayed their trust and ruled tyrannically.

By then, another monarch, James II had been ousted. Monarchy was restored only when the future King William III agreed to respect the authority of Parliament and the people, as set down in the Bill of Rights (1689). With the monarch's power limited by this constitutional arrangement, the country became a *constitutional monarchy*. It is still referred to as such today – though since the monarch's powers are now even more restricted and the main authority resides in a Parliament elected by the general public, it would be more accurate to call modern Britain a *constitutional democracy*.

Constitutional republicanism

John Locke's ideas were highly influential on the founders of what would become the United States of America. Like him, they rejected the arbitrary power of monarchs – listing the 'abuses and usurpations' of King George III at length in the *Declaration of Independence* (1776). They stressed political equality, but still feared that democracy would be dangerous because it could easily descend into mob rule. They debated the matter, concluding that popular involvement in public affairs was only one part of good government. What they needed was a *republic* – a government carefully constructed according to rules and principles, where decisions would be made by representatives elected by the people, but where those representatives would be bound by the same laws as everyone else, with their powers being limited and defined in a written constitution.

> Democracy is not freedom. Democracy is two wolves and a lamb voting on what to have for lunch. Freedom comes from the recognition of certain rights which may not be taken, not even by a 99% vote.
>
> — Marvin Simkin (1992), 'Individual Rights', *Los Angeles Times*

The French philosopher Montesquieu (1748) had argued that democracy could never work well because people put their own interests over the general interest. In particular, those given power would abuse it – a point of particular concern to Locke, the Americans, and many that followed them. The only antidote to the abuse of power by those in authority, thought Montesquieu, was *checks and balances*: to check all power with balancing power. And forty years later, these ideas informed the new Constitution of the United States, with its separation of powers, electoral colleges, limits on authority, and other devices aimed at creating a *limited* representative government. (Although these political rights and protections were not extended to the 800,000 or so slaves and indigenous people living there at the time).

Things were different again in France. There, the Reign of Terror (1793–94) that followed the 1789 Revolution confirmed to America's founders that they were right to be worried about democracy's potential slide into chaos. The

French revolutionaries' belief that their elective oligarchy could be guided by the 'general will' of the public was mistaken; there was only disagreement and argument, backed up by violence. The Terror led the English political theorist Edmund Burke (1790) to complain, in his *Reflections on the Revolution in France*, that: 'In a democracy, the majority of the citizens is capable of exercising the most cruel oppressions upon the minority'.

Liberal democracy

In 1835, another French thinker, Alexis de Tocqueville, published *Democracy in America*. The apparent success of the American republic, he concluded, was not due solely to its decentralisation, its balance of powers, its devolved authority ('federalism'), and other constitutional features, crucial though these were. America's moral and social culture, he thought, was vital too. Civil society – America's profusion of churches, charities, clubs, self-help groups, and community associations – served to educate and moderate the voting public. Common interest and decency, he concluded, could restrain the slide into mob rule; but they had to be part of the culture in order to work.

The great nineteenth-century English philosopher John Stuart Mill went on to lay out the principles of modern liberal democracy (1861). Like the Greeks, he feared the tyranny of an ignorant, fickle majority led by vested interests and charismatic demagogues. Nor was direct democracy feasible in his world, where communities were much larger than ancient Athens and it was impossible to get all citizens together. The only workable system for modern times, he thought, would be *representative* government. But the representatives should not be mere *delegates*, appointed merely to echo their voters' prejudices. Rather, they should think and act independently and responsibly, even if that meant rejecting the popular opinion. As Edmund Burke (1774) had put it earlier, in his 'Speech to the Electors of Bristol': 'Your representative owes you, not his industry only, but his judgement; and he betrays, instead of serving you, if he sacrifices it to your opinion'.

Yet in any system of government, the rights and liberties of individuals come first and must be protected, insisted Mill. He did not think that rights were somehow God-given or part of our nature, as Locke and the Americans had. He thought they were moral rules that we followed because they worked. And a government can work and endure only if it respects those rights and protects its citizens' lives, freedom and property. In *On Liberty*, Mill (1859) outlined just how limited he thought government interventions should be. Even if there were an overwhelming majority in favour of restricting people's actions, 'The only purpose for which power can be rightfully exercised over any member of a civilized community, against his will, is to prevent harm to others'.

The expansion of democracy...

By now the principles of liberal democracy were starting to coalesce, even if Britain's own Parliament remained far from democratic. But the growing liberalism of the 1800s produced demands to end the corrupt electoral system – in which only larger property owners could vote, where some landowners controlled entire parliamentary districts, and where bribery, corruption and intimidation were rife. The Great Reform Act of 1832 helped improve things, though its main impact was in widening the electorate, with smaller landowners and leaseholders now given the vote. Another reform, in 1867, widened the franchise even more, to include 'respectable' working men of modest incomes.

It would be many more years before women could vote in England – and indeed most other countries. The pioneers of female suffrage were on the other side of the world, in New Zealand and Australia (although indigenous Australians were still excluded in some states until as late as 1965). Finland and Norway let women vote before World War I, as Austria, Germany, Poland, Russia, the Netherlands, the US and Sweden did shortly after. The UK extended the vote to female property owners in 1918, then more generally in 1928. But women in Portugal and Switzerland had to wait until the 1970s; and there are some countries where women are still excluded from elections.

... beyond its limits?

The widening of the franchise, from propertied males to all citizens, increased the legitimacy of representative government (now universally called 'democracy') and boosted the idea that this method should be used over a wider range of issues. This expansion coincided with an upsurge in general prosperity, which helped the case for yet further expansion (though the economic upturn was perhaps due more to increased adoption of liberal ideas such as free trade and open markets, than to popular voting).

The twentieth century saw this more-legitimised 'democracy' spread into many more parts of life, replacing individual choices in such areas as healthcare, education, pension savings and charitable giving by collective ones. As government expanded, there were more and more opportunities for interest groups to use their influence to gain special privileges, grants, subsidies, tax concessions and other benefits. By the end of the century, a political elite had sprung up, comprising politicians, lobbyists, those in NGOs, commissions, tribunals, regulatory agencies, quangos, political media, think tanks and others – from whose attention few parts of individual life were exempt.

> Imagine if all of life were determined by majority rule. Every meal would be a pizza. Every pair of pants ... would be stone-washed denim. Celebrity diet and exercise books would be the only thing on the shelves at the library.
> — P. J. O'Rourke (1991), *Parliament of Whores*

The death of democracy?

Despite the apparent legitimacy of representative government, some critics see its reality as one of abject failure. To them, what we have created is not democracy but an elective populist oligarchy, whose self-interest, short-term focus and lack of principle allows government to expand unchecked, breeding bureaucracy, cronyism and reckless overspending – as well as crushing individual liberty under majority opinion. They complain that many ordinary people have come to regard politics as either irrelevant to them or out of their control – an alienation that makes it even easier for the political class to exploit them. (As Pericles told the Athenians, just because you are not interested in politics does not mean that politics is not interested in you.)

Nevertheless, life and politics in relatively liberal democracies remain far freer and more open than in the oligarchies of earlier times. Yet the democratic ideal can certainly be corrupted, and not just by neglect. Even in our supposedly enlightened age today, governments that claim to be 'democratic' still commonly engage in vote-rigging, disenfranchisement, censorship, confiscation, arbitrary arrest, the politicisation of the courts and detention without trial. The first priority in changing that is to be clear about what democracy really means and what institutions and principles underpin it.

3 DEMOCRATIC INSTITUTIONS

While nearly all governments claim to be democracies, enjoying the legitimacy that this suggests, very few live up to the ideal. Supposedly 'democratic' regimes rig elections, stifle criticism by controlling the media, employ the police and courts to persecute opponents, and abuse the legal and financial power of the state to enrich themselves and their cronies. A report by the Economist Intelligence Unit (2019) concluded that only 22 countries, home to just 5.7 per cent of the world's population, could legitimately be called 'full' democracies, and 15 of those were in Western Europe. Indeed, countries that put 'democratic republic' in their official names (such as Algeria, Ethiopia, North Korea, Laos and Nepal) tend to be among the most authoritarian.

It is important, therefore, that we should maintain a clear idea of what democracy really is, rather than being deceived by authoritarian regimes that misrepresent themselves as democratic, either deliberately or out of self-delusion. We need to map out the core principles of democracy so we can separate real democracies from sham ones.

The purpose and power of government

To start the process, we might first ask what the purpose of *government* is, and then ask how democracy assists that purpose.

The answer given by Locke, Mill and other liberal theorists is that, although human beings are social creatures and mostly get along together, they can often be coerced by people who are willing to use force to dominate, rob or defraud them. Having a government allows individuals to maximise their freedom by discouraging the use of force through an organised system of justice. Government therefore has no independent life and identity of its own: it exists solely to provide citizens with security and protect their freedom.

Citizens need to give government certain powers to achieve these aims – the ability to use force to detain and punish offenders, for example. That does not mean that the government needs to wield enormous force: but what power it has must be wielded on behalf of the people. Government force cannot be used to control them – that would negate its entire purpose. The arrangement must be *consensual*. And since government's decisions affect everyone, everyone should be involved in the process, their views counting equally. Hence the need for some kind of democratic decision-making system.

Power tends to corrupt, and absolute power corrupts absolutely. Great men are almost always bad men, even when they exercise influence and not authority; still more when you superadd the tendency or the certainty of corruption by authority.

— Lord Acton (1887), *Letter to Bishop Creighton*

But since government *does* have coercive power, there remains the threat that those in the majority could use that power against others. Indeed, given that human beings are self-interested, we should presume that they would. 'In contriving a system of government', warned the eighteenth-century Scottish philosopher David Hume (1758), 'every man ought to be supposed a knave, and to have no other end ... than private interest'. Two hundred years later, in his wartime book *The Road to Serfdom*, the Anglo-Austrian thinker F. A. Hayek (1944) charted how easily a democracy could slide into the gang rule of totalitarian dictatorship. And, indeed, during the 2020 Covid-19 pandemic, many citizens of democratic countries were surprised by the powers their politicians had to impose sweeping restrictions on the conduct of everyday life.

If unchecked, majority rule gives minorities and individuals no protection against the self-interest of the majority in power. Hence, there is an argument for a limited, *liberal democracy* in which individuals' basic rights and freedoms always trump any majority decision, and where government intervenes only in order to preserve them (Butler 2013). These limitations may be specified formally in a constitution.

However, some theorists believe the threat of democracy drifting into oppression, though real, is overstated. For example, the Turkish-American economist Daron

Acemoglu and his British colleague James Robinson (2006) found that democracy can and does survive where the political institutions, economic system and civil society are strong. Likewise, the political scientists André Alves and John Meadowcroft (2014) found that, in fact, moderate democracies with mixed (state and private) economic systems are both widespread and stable – while totalitarian systems struggle to survive in the long term. Quite simply, they argue, there is a practical limit to the size of a ruling gang and its cronies, since the more numerous the exploiters become, the fewer (and less motivated) productive citizens there are to exploit.

The key role of democracy

As well as democracy being an arguably *fair way to make collective choices*, theorists have supported it for other reasons. Some claim that democracy is *good in itself* because it is the only system of government based on moral and political equality. Others say it produces *good outcomes* such as social participation, personal responsibility, peace or prosperity. The evidence on all these is debatable.

Yet there is one clear benefit of democracy that is often overlooked. We tend to think of democracy mainly as a way of *electing* our decision-makers. But its real importance is in *restraining* them – and *removing* them peacefully. After all, legislators are not angels: they are human beings, like the rest of us. They are easily tempted and corrupted by power. In office, they may begin to put their own interests above ours. Or perhaps, as time goes on, their views (or ours) change and we feel that they no longer properly represent us. Whatever the reason, our ability to remove people from office at elections helps prevent them from accumulating and abusing power and keeps them focused on the public that they are supposed to represent. As the twentieth-century Anglo-Austrian philosopher Sir Karl Popper put it (1945): 'it is not at all easy to get a government on whose goodness and wisdom one can implicitly rely. ... [This] forces us to replace the question: *Who should rule?* by the new question: *How can we so organize political institutions that bad or incompetent rulers can be prevented from doing too much damage?*' [italics in original].

Direct democracy

Democracy, as we have seen, can be *direct* or *representative*. In *direct democracy*, the general public decide directly on political issues (such as tax rates, defence or welfare policy). But direct democracy is rare today.

One place that direct democracy does survive is in Switzerland. There, most political power resides in the 27 cantons and 3,000 communes, rather than in the federal government. The cantons vary in size, from Zurich, with a population of 1.5 million, to Appenzell Innerhoden, with only 16,000. Referendums are common and the smaller cantons use citizens' assemblies. Another example is the Town Meetings held in about 1,000 New England towns. Going back to the seventeenth century, these assemblies rule over local matters such as highways, licensing and budgets – though the exact mix varies. Some, however, have mutated into representative bodies, with larger towns electing delegates to attend Town Meetings, rather than everyone attending. And modern nation states too are simply too large for their citizens to gather in law-making assemblies. They might occasionally hold *referendums* – where the entire electorate can vote on a particular issue – but this is a cumbersome way to make detailed decisions on the complex issues facing a modern state.

Some activists argue that modern democracy could be made more direct through online voting. But there would still have to be limits on what the majority could legitimately decide. And there are doubts whether the public have sufficient interest and stamina for researching policies and taking a constant stream of difficult political decisions.

Representative democracy

For reasons like these, the current norm is *representative democracy* – where the public do not generally make the laws themselves, but elect representatives (such as mayors, parliamentarians and presidents) to decide laws and policies on their behalf.

Critics argue that this is not genuine democracy, any more than hiring a house painter is the same as painting the house yourself; and that the only role of the public is the very limited one of choosing those who will run things. But at least the public are involved in that choice, rather than having rulers imposed upon them; and they remain free to get involved more deeply, such as standing for office and participating in the ongoing public debate.

In addition, many representative systems today still retain elements of direct public control, such as *referendums* (where the general public vote on key issues), *petitions* and *initiatives* (where groups of voters can force a vote in parliament or call a referendum), *term limits* (where representatives can hold office for no more than a set time), and *recall* (where voters can eject a representative from office). But, in general, many voters prefer to leave everyday politics up to people who have more time, judgement and interest in it, rather than having to consider every issue themselves.

So, when people speak of 'democracy' today, they usually mean *representative government,* and this has become the modern meaning of the word. This use does, however, generate confusion. It bundles into one word a wide variety of different systems. It also suggests that the virtues of direct democracy (such as public participation in law-making) also exist in representative systems, even though in some such systems, the general public have little or no genuine say at all.

Liberal democracy

Within the very wide range of representative systems lies *liberal democracy.* Liberal democracies are representative systems that are subject to classical liberal principles. Most importantly, they demand that individual rights – such as the rights to life, liberty and property – must always be respected: no 'democratic' decision can override them. But, more broadly, the countries that are often described as liberal democracies commonly share other features that help achieve this protection, such as accepted legal rules on how decisions are made, constitutional limits on government, the separation of legislative and executive power, and an independent justice system. They also open up to public engagement in public affairs, such as free and fair elections in which anyone can stand for office, competing parties, independent media, and open political debate.

Beyond that, they differ in many ways. Some examples of relatively liberal democracy are *constitutional monarchies* (for example, Denmark, Japan, Spain and the UK) – governments nominally headed by a monarch, but a monarch whose power is limited by constitutional rules. Others are *republics* (for example, France, Ireland and the US), where leaders are elected, but their power is also constitutionally limited. And in each system, the different constitutional elements – such as the head of state (for example, monarch or president) and the various parliamentary chambers (for example, Senate or House of Deputies) and branches of government (executive, legislative and judicial) – may have different degrees of power.

Liberal democracy is not easy to get right. How it should work and which rights and freedoms it should prioritise over majority decision-making are complex and controversial questions. For instance, it seems obvious that the majority in a liberal democracy should not have power to arbitrarily arrest, imprison or exile a minority they disagree with; but can they legitimately tax minorities – and impose higher taxes on rich people, say? Are they permitted to intervene in people's lifestyles (such as limiting their consumption of narcotics, alcohol or sugar) in the hope of saving citizens from self-harm? Or dictate people's economic choices (such as where they live or work) in the national interest? Should the authorities in a liberal democracy be able to suspend certain freedoms in times of war or pandemic, or spy on their citizens' communications in order to help combat the threat of terrorism?

There are no simple yes/no answers to such questions. Though liberal democracy is remarkably resilient, its future can be assured only if there is a general understanding of the principles that underpin it.

4 THE PRINCIPLES OF DEMOCRACY

The essentials of liberal democracy

When we look at the countries that are often described as examples of liberal democracy, certain features and institutions stand out.

Wide franchise. Liberal democracy rests on a *wide franchise and equal political status*: nearly all adults are eligible to vote and their votes count equally. Children and adults with serious mental disabilities may be excluded as incompetent to vote; and in some countries prison inmates (and even released felons) may be excluded on the grounds that their criminality makes them unfit to participate in social affairs. Otherwise, all citizens are included.

However, exactly who counts as a citizen is a matter of debate. Once, only propertied males were seen as having sufficient stake in a country to vote responsibly. For similar reasons, some people today would deny the vote to recent immigrants and temporary residents.

Another problem is that a territory may be occupied by different populations, divided by their sense of nationhood (for example, Russians in Ukraine), language (for example, French speakers in Canada), race (for example, in Southern

Africa), or religion (for example, in Somalia, Bosnia, Iraq, Pakistan and many others). Each group may reject the right of the others to make collective decisions that affect them. Liberal principles would make the definition of citizenship as inclusive as possible; but citizenship rules also have to be clear and generally accepted – which may be hard to achieve.

Open elections. Liberal democracies allow anyone to run for public office. Again, children, prisoners or those with mental disabilities might be excluded. But people are not excluded as candidates because of their particular party, religion, class, family, ethnic group or gender. Nor are those in power entitled to rule their opponents as unfit for office. A liberal democracy trusts its citizens to make their own decisions about who is fit to represent them.

Elections in a liberal democracy are *frequent*, *free* and *fair*. On *frequency*, different countries have different views on how often the elections for different offices should be held. The US, for example, elects representatives every two years, presidents every four, and senators every six. France elected its president every seven years until a 2000 referendum shortened it to five. And many places put limits on the number of terms that elected officers can serve. What matters is that elections are frequent enough, and terms of office short enough, first to prevent anyone accumulating autocratic power, and second to convince the defeated side that it is worth waiting peacefully until the next election rather than resorting to violence.

Free elections are ones where electors can vote, and choose who to vote for, without being intimidated. That in turn requires the use of genuine secret ballots. Liberal democracies often employ independent oversight panels to ensure that these conditions are met.

Fair elections are those where individuals and parties have an equal right to seek election, to campaign and hold peaceful meetings, where electoral boundaries are decided objectively by independent panels (not by the politicians in power), where votes are counted accurately and where those votes determine the outcome. Yet countries have different views on the specifics of what counts as 'fair'. The UK has low limits on election spending, for example, but not on donations to political parties; while the US has limits on donations but not on spending.

Free debate. Free and fair elections work only if issues can be freely raised and debated. That implies a right to free speech – including the right to criticise those in power without being charged with sedition or otherwise intimidated. It implies a free media, not controlled by the state for the benefit of those in power. And it requires people to be able to access accurate information about government – not a state monopoly on official information.

Honest representation. Those taking office must be genuinely accountable to the public – with independent and impartial courts, judges and officials to whom citizens can appeal if they believe that representatives are exceeding their powers or violating people's rights. There might even be recall provisions to remove legislators at any time if their electors decide that they have abused their position.

And in line with the key purpose of elections, representatives must respect election results and be prepared to stand down when they are voted out. After all, part of the purpose of liberal democracy is to make political transitions possible and peaceful. State power cannot be used to help incumbents stay in office; on the contrary, it should be used to ensure that electors' choices are respected.

Rights and principles. It is also important that the basic rights of individuals are known, generally accepted, respected, and legally guaranteed such that no electoral majority can override them. Whether these rights are seen as an inherent part of being human, or are adopted because they seem to work, there must be broad agreement on what rights people should have, and a general commitment to protecting them.

Certainly, different liberal democracies have slightly different views on what those basic rights should be. All agree that everyone has the right to life, liberty, the pursuit of personal happiness, and the ownership of property. But the precise rules – for example, what you are or are not allowed to build on your land, or the offences which might justify the authorities imprisoning you – might vary.

Constitutions. Most liberal democracies have written constitutions that protect people's basic rights, specify the limits on elective power and provide for mechanisms such as the separation of powers to keep it in check. However, the constitution may not exist as a single document: in the UK, for example, various laws and conventions from Magna Carta through the Bill of Rights to the Parliament Act and Devolution Acts define people's core rights and how the government should operate.

To ensure that a majority cannot simply tear up such protections, most constitutions require a large majority and careful process before they can be changed. Amendments to the US Constitution, for example, require two-thirds majorities in the Senate and House of Representatives, plus three-quarters of the state legislators to approve. The UK is an exception: theoretically Parliament can amend any part of its constitutional structure – though normally any such proposal is subject to a very long and exacting public debate.

Ultimately, though, not even a written constitution will safeguard individual rights and freedoms: that needs a deep cultural and intellectual commitment among the general population.

Desirable elements of liberal representation

Participation. In addition to these essential features, there are other desirable ones. For example, it is thought beneficial to have a culture of *wide*, *active* and *voluntary participation* in the democratic process. This allows different ideas to be aired and adds to the legitimacy of the process – though liberals note that what legitimises democracy is not maximising *political engagement* but maximising *individual freedom and security*.

Candidates. Political parties are a useful feature of democracy because they give electors a 'brand' to latch on to. But this again needs restraint: if parties try to control their brands too tightly (for example, by dictating each candidate's election platform and 'whipping' their votes in parliament), candidates lose their independence and the public are denied their judgement. This suggests that candidates *should be chosen openly*, rather than by party lists of approved candidates (which further consolidate party insiders' grip on politics).

Federalism. Ideally, decisions should be devolved to the lowest level possible, so that those making the choices are those who are affected by them, not distant people with little grasp of local circumstances. But some central restraint on local decisions is desirable. For example, if a particular locality is dominated by an ethnic or religious group, as is often the case, minorities may be oppressed by the majority. Over a larger area, opinions are likely to be more mixed and minorities are therefore more likely to be respected and protected.

Civic toleration. Underpinning all of this, however, liberal democracy works best where there is toleration of diverse views, social and economic stability, and peace.

It remains questionable how many of these desirable features actually prevail in the majority of countries that claim to be 'democracies' today.

The operation of liberal democracy

Justice. As we have seen, liberal democracy exists primarily to defend and expand personal freedom and to protect individuals from coercion. It therefore requires a justice system to deter and punish the use of fraud and force – including the abuse of power by those in authority.

For this to work, *laws must be principled, clear and relatively stable* so that they can be generally understood. They need to be broadly predictable, not arbitrary, and it must be feasible to obey them. The process of justice itself must also be principled and predictable, following 'due process of law', with (for example) no arbitrary arrest and detention, and with accused individuals having the right to know the charges against them, face their accusers in a fair trial, and remain silent without that counting against them.

To further protect individual rights and freedoms, the police, courts and judges must be independent – not controlled by and promoting the interests of those in political power. For example, if rulers are suspected of stealing public funds, the justice system needs to be able to pursue fearlessly the appropriate enquiries and prosecutions. And if the rulers seek to alter or misinterpret the constitution to serve their own interests, that must be countered too.

Property rights. Liberal democracy regards the ownership and use of property not just as a basic right but as a bastion against coercion and a driver of economic progress. A person who has invested time and energy in creating property has the right to use and enjoy it. The justice system therefore protects people's property just as it protects their person. The exact rules may vary between different countries, but individuals must be able to *exclude* others from using their property, *use* their property freely themselves, and *transfer* it by gift or sale. These rules must be enforceable in the courts.

Taxation. The protection of freedom requires a defence and a justice system, and taxation seems a reasonable way to pay for them. But this does mean that people's property – in this case, their money – must be taken from them, by a state that is supposed to preserve it. Relying on voluntary contributions would open up a 'free rider' problem, where some people would enjoy states' services without paying. If compulsory payments are the only feasible option, a liberal democracy ensures that taxes are low and used only for preserving the rights and security of citizens. However, the ease with which majorities could use taxes to exploit minorities (such as 'the rich') has led some liberals, such as the American political economists Geoffrey Brennan and James Buchanan (1980), to argue that taxation should be limited in size, structured to prevent abuse, and undertaken only with near-unanimous consent.

Personal freedom. As John Stuart Mill pointed out, governments have no authority over people's lives, freedoms and property except to achieve the limited ends of security and freedom. If government's function is to protect freedom, any curbs on individual liberty must be fully justified in advance. The government cannot restrict people's actions arbitrarily or without full consideration.

Importantly, full consideration of public policy means that individuals must have the right to think and speak as they please, including being able to criticise the law and the government without fear of censorship or punishment. They must be free to assemble together, form political parties and campaign in elections. These things are crucial to the operation of a liberal democracy; any restrictions on them should be extensively justified.

Likewise, people should be able to live as they choose. Government exists to protect our freedoms, not to dictate our lifestyle. Also, having a diversity of ideas and ways of living to draw on helps society to grow, develop and survive. And the freedom to control your own life is essential for personal and moral development and learning. A nation of ciphers controlled by the authorities is unlikely to progress, or to survive in a changing world.

Because freedom and security are the principal functions of government, we have every right to remove a government that does not deliver them – especially one that actively violates them. Ideally, that should be through peaceful means, which is why liberal democracies have elections. But we still retain the right to defend ourselves and our property from abuse by others, even by the state. A peaceful political or social order is based on trust, cooperation and communication: not on force, but freedom.

Economic freedom. Economic freedom is inseparable from personal freedom. A state that controls the economic resources controls life. A state that controls the media, owns the meeting venues, censors publishing, and restricts travel can shut down public criticism and debate.

Economic freedom is in any case a surer way to prosperity than political control of economic resources. As the British author Matt Ridley (2020) points out, individual innovation and entrepreneurship, and the application of many minds, are essential if goods and services are to become cheaper and better. A free economy can adjust to change much quicker than a controlled one.

5 REPRESENTATIVE DEMOCRACIES TODAY

Parliamentary government

Legislative and executive power. For most of history, legislative assemblies were aristocratic bodies: the idea that they might be *elected* by and *represent* the general public is much more recent. Britain's Parliament, for example, grew out of a council of barons who sought to curb the king's power. Gradually, non-aristocratic landowners were added as members, but the purpose of medieval parliaments was still to protect people with property against kingly power, not to benefit the common people.

After further confrontations, much of the monarch's ancient power was taken over by Parliament itself. And Britain exported this *parliamentary government* – where executive and legislative power is still not separated but where premiers and ministers sit in the legislature – to other countries (including many former colonies now in the Commonwealth).

One benefit of this model is that ministers are directly accountable to electors. However, having the executive in Parliament undermines its role of protecting the public from executive power. Conversely, a US-style division of powers allows the executive to be chosen from a much wider pool of expertise, and its power to be checked by an independent legislature; but then ministers become more distant from, and less accountable to, the public.

Unicameral and bicameral. Most liberal democracies have evolved *bicameral* (two-chamber) legislatures. Having two legislative chambers allows each to question and restrain the actions of the other. Their differences have to be resolved before laws are passed, making it harder to abuse the rights of individuals or small groups. (However, some countries with a single-chamber *unicameral* legislature, such as Norway, Iceland, Denmark, Sweden or New Zealand, respect individual rights strongly; while some others with a two-chamber *bicameral* legislature, such as Russia or Zimbabwe, perhaps have less respect for such ideals.)

If the members of each chamber are chosen by different methods, it can bring a wider range of viewpoints into the public debate. For example, the US elects representatives on roughly equal population areas; but each state elects only two senators, regardless of its size; this helps ensure that the interests of smaller states are heard. Australian senators are elected by the *single transferable vote* system, which produces a greater diversity in that chamber than the *instant run-off* or *preferential voting* system used in the House of Representatives.

Presidential systems

Where legislative power is separated from executive power, the executive is often led by a president. The president's role varies. In some countries such as Ireland, it is largely ceremonial. In others, such as the US, the president wields strong executive powers: among other things, the US president is empowered to nominate ministers and officials, propose budgets, veto legislation, negotiate treaties and even conduct wars.

Presidents may be elected by popular ballot or chosen by legislators. However, if they are elected on a wide popular franchise, they have the independence and legitimacy to block legislative measures that might threaten the freedom and security of the public at large – an additional, useful restraint on power.

Constitutional monarchies

A surprising number of liberal democracies are actually *constitutional monarchies* – in which, as already mentioned, the monarch's powers are limited by conventional or written constitutional rules. They include the UK and Commonwealth countries such as Australia, New Zealand and Canada. Europe too has limited monarchies such as Belgium, Denmark, the Netherlands and Spain.

The exact powers of these monarchs vary. But even largely ceremonial monarchs (as most are) may still wield some authority. During Spain's attempted coup in 1981, for example, the newly restored king, Juan Carlos, ordered the military back to barracks – successfully. The crucial importance of constitutional monarchs may not be the power they possess, but the power they deny to other people, such as army officers, judges and politicians.

The role of the public

Many critics see 'voter ignorance' as a fundamental flaw in democracy. But electors do not need to consider and understand the details of every policy themselves: their task is only to elect representatives who will do that for them. A party label, indicating a candidate's broad stance on the issues, may be all the information that electors require.

For electors, representative systems have advantages over 'participative' systems that involve everyone in decision-making. Electors may be busy with their own concerns and have little time or interest in political debates; so, it makes sense to pass the task onto someone who does. And electors may well believe that the legislators they choose have greater expertise and better political judgement than they do themselves.

What then restrains politicians from abusing the decision-making power that electors give them? Short of revolution, it is the threat of electoral defeat. Again, the public's key role in democracy is not to *choose* leaders but to *remove them*.

It is true that the public may well prefer strong leaders, and hand them great powers; but no leader can long remain strong if they lose the consent of the people. With free and fair elections, changes in leadership can come peacefully.

And with free speech, open debate and honest elections, politicians have to compete for public approval and consent, and make a good case for being returned to office.

Safeguarding the process

Voting is not a very significant act for an individual, though in a democracy it decides who does – or does not – form a government. But with government comes power, so there is always a threat that vested interest groups and political factions may use fraud, bribery, coercion, vote-rigging and other illicit means to sway election results. Most worryingly, those in office may try to manipulate election boundaries, use state resources to influence voters, use state media to undermine candidates, deploy the police, army and courts against their rivals, or simply lie about the number of votes cast for each candidate.

A liberal democracy needs mechanisms to resist these threats, such as independent boundary and election commissions, international scrutiny of elections, rules on candidates' use of state resources and state media, and punishment for election fraud. However, the best restraint is a culture that rejects such corruption.

Electoral systems

There are many different electoral systems, and commentators often have strong views on which one produces the 'best' outcomes. But what is 'best' is a matter of opinion; in reality, each system has both strengths and weaknesses.

First past the post (FPTP) is a common system, in which the candidate with the most votes gets elected. It is simple, easy to understand, quick and produces clear results. It also provides electors with a single representative to go to if they have problems with the government or want to express their views. On the other hand, if the votes cast are split between many candidates, someone with only minority support can be elected. The system favours two-party politics, which may not capture the full spread of public opinion. And if the electoral districts are small, the system often produces 'safe' seats, giving voters on the losing side no real electoral power at all.

To ease these problems, various systems of *proportional representation* have been devised. One is the *alternative vote* method. Voters rank the candidates in order of preference, and the candidates with the least votes are eliminated one by one, with their second preferences awarded to the others, until one achieves an overall majority. The advantage is that everyone's preference counts – at least to some degree. But then the system is complicated to understand and administer. It favours third-party candidates more than FPTP, but then this can give a foothold to extremist parties.

A variant is to have multi-member constituencies, which can be larger and therefore less prone to becoming 'safe' for one party, with candidates elected by a *single transferable vote* (STV) system, in which losing candidates are eliminated until the number of candidates matches the number of seats. But this is even more complicated to understand and operate. It can also leave voters unsure who represents them. Candidates may be more interested in getting on a party list than appealing to voters.

Unfortunately, proportional systems like these often produce governments built on 'coalitions of convenience' (often involving small extremist parties), which may not reflect public opinion and can be hard to remove. On the other hand, FPTP and other non-proportional systems run the risk of under-representing third parties.

Many other variants are common, such as *mixed member systems* in which, if a party receives a large share of the national vote but wins few seats, it is given additional seats allocated from a party list of candidates. But again, this produces candidates who are more focused on getting a high place on a party list than appealing to voters.

For presidential elections, America employs the *electoral college* system. Electors do not vote directly for the president, but for local candidates who in turn vote to choose the president. This is designed to prevent the electorates in very large states from overwhelming those in smaller ones, ensuring that every part of the country is counted; but it also means that a president can be elected on only a minority of the votes cast, as Donald Trump was in 2016 and George W. Bush was in 2000.

To conclude, there is no unquestionably 'fair' voting system. But if the electoral system as a whole is open, fair and allows change, then at least the losers might accept defeat and be willing to wait for another chance, rather than taking up arms.

Accountability to the public

Liberal democracies – uniquely – are held to public account in many different ways. For example, the legislature can delay or obstruct executive action. The courts can ensure that decisions are taken and executed legally, and that people's rights are protected. The media and independent experts can debate the wisdom of government policies. Electors can punish governments at the polls. American-style primaries and other selection measures can help ensure that candidates are genuinely fit for office. Referendums and ballot initiatives can provide a further restraint on those in power. Federalism, in which power is exercised at the lowest level possible (the lowest being the individual), allows people to escape from distant and oppressive authority. And many kinds of citizens' groups have a strong voice in the national debate.

A constitution is a useful further restraint and can provide a valuable guarantee of individuals' basic rights and freedoms. But the process of drawing up a constitution needs care: it can be easily dominated by ruling parties or hijacked by ideologues and interest groups that seek to shape political institutions for their own benefit.

The tension between democracy and rights

Democracy is inevitably a balance between individual rights and the majority will. Liberal democracy gives rights the priority. But the exact balance will never be stable, because there will never be full agreement on the details. What people have a right to do or say in public, or build on their land, or spend their money on (such as gambling, prostitution, drugs or alcohol) are matters of debate. Rights are not indisputable: they are a political expression of moral principles – on which people disagree. The task for liberals is to guarantee that, as far as possible, the supposed legitimacy of majority decisions is not allowed to smother the freedoms of the minority – and ultimately, of everyone.

6 THE BENEFITS OF DEMOCRACY

Preventing the accumulation of power

Perhaps the greatest benefit of liberal democracy is that it enables the public to change their leaders peacefully, without having to resort to violence. For autocratic regimes, the threat of rebellion and revolution is always a major concern, and they typically maintain large armies to prevent it. But such military might may also be used more generally to stifle criticism and consolidate power.

Frequent changes in leadership, by contrast, help prevent leaders or political factions from accumulating and consolidating power. And even if a government becomes unpopular, it is still less likely to build up repressive forces because the threat of violent revolution is lower when elections are frequent. With peace prevailing, human effort and attention can then be turned to more productive and enriching activities.

Absorbing change

Liberal democracies are adaptive. They are able to adjust to changes in events, and in public attitudes. They can do this better than most other systems, because they are not bound by some single view or ideology or set of prejudices about how society should function. Ideology and prejudice promote a set way of doing things, and resist any change or deviation from that; but liberal democracy embraces change and puts it to good use. For example, democracy tolerates many different ideas and lifestyles. So, when circumstances change, we have plenty of practical options around that can help us overcome, absorb, divert or use the changes to our advantage. And over the years, the public's opinion may change on many important issues – such as immigration, welfare provision, the need for military intervention or transgender rights; democratic debates and decisions simply change along with those movements. Democracy is a system for any kind of society.

With liberal democracies' tolerance, openness, diversity and flair for compromise, they may look much weaker and less focused than autocratic regimes when faced with major threats and upheavals such as wars and natural disasters. But these same qualities also give them surprising resilience and strength – as fascist and other autocratic leaders have discovered in the past.

Speaking to our values

Another benefit that many commentators see in liberal democracy is that it embraces and enshrines important human values, such as the political equality of individuals. However much they may differ in other ways, such as income or wealth, every citizen can participate in the electoral process. They are free to be voters, party members, candidates or campaigners without fear of discrimination or repression. It does not matter whether they are rich or poor, skilled or unskilled, urban or rural, high-born or low, or whatever their ethnicity or religion or colour or class or family or views on politics might be. Politically, their views count equally.

Other observers praise the fact that democracy may encourage participation in society – or at the very least, it does not exclude anyone from participating in politics because some person in government believes them to be unqualified, undeserving, disruptive or treasonous. Nor is the population in a democracy divided into those considered fit to rule and those considered fit only to be ruled – a remarkably common prejudice in other regimes. Under liberal democracy, everyone is free to become an active citizen and stand for office, and the wide mass of the people decide which are best for it.

This widespread involvement in social affairs fosters citizens' intellectual, moral and political development too, say its supporters. It gives people both the opportunity and the incentive to think about and debate political and moral choices, and which policy actions might best resolve them.

Promoting honest policy

Liberal democracy means that we live under governments and laws that we choose ourselves – at least to some extent – rather than under the power of leaders who are imposed on us. This reduces the use of force in society and the need to coerce people into accepting autocratic government decisions. It is a more consensual and peaceable method of political change.

The fair and free elections and open government that are a part of liberal democracy also promote accountability and transparency among those standing for or elected into office. As politicians compete for the approval of the public in elections, their record, abilities and character all come under scrutiny. Or as the American H. L. Mencken (1956) impishly put it: 'Under democracy one party always devotes its chief energies to trying to prove that the other party is unfit to rule – and both commonly succeed and are right'. But in addition to the sparring between parties, candidates will be looked at closely by electors; their shortcomings will be readily pointed out by others; they will face probing by the media and social media; and interest groups will tackle them on their policy stances.

Dishonesty is punished, too. If citizens come to believe that those they elected are corrupt, inadequate or have made bad decisions, they can vote to remove them – either at the next election or, in some countries, by a recall petition. In autocratic systems, by contrast, bad leaders cannot be removed easily; and those in power will often cling to it, and to their policies too, even if they are failing.

Criticism and progress

The toleration that is one of liberal democracy's key principles allows open criticism of a country's leadership – something that is not always wise nor even possible under some autocratic regimes. Immune from criticism, auto-crats can hush up scandals and ensure that their mistakes are concealed or ignored. It is often said that parliaments are merely talking shops, but the ability to talk freely in such an open forum is crucial in exposing leaders and their ideas to questioning. That public debate then informs voters when they hold their leaders to account at the next election.

That is also an important factor in human progress. It is clearly an advantage if new public policy proposals – and indeed, any ideas on any subject – can be tested in open debate, where people can point out their strengths and weaknesses. That allows potentially good ideas to be improved, and weaker ones to be amended or abandoned before they cause damage. By harnessing the 'wisdom of crowds', say its supporters, democracy can make better policy decisions than systems in which the decisions of the authorities are not challenged and tested in open debate.

Protecting individual rights

Bruce Bueno de Mesquita and his colleagues (2003) found that countries with high-quality democratic institutions score well in terms of defending human rights. It may not be that democracy automatically generates these benefits; it may be that the countries that value rights most believe democracy defends them best. Either way, liberal democra-cies usually have the strongest protections on rights such as life, liberty, property ownership, free association, free speech, and equal participation in the political process.

Although democratic systems and the respect of rights usually go together, there remains a tension between the will of the majority and the rights of individuals. The majority, and their elected politicians, may well believe that there are good reasons to curb people's rights. For example, they may decide that, in order to save the public from the threat of terrorism, the police and security authorities should be empowered to arrest and hold individuals for long periods, conduct random street and house searches, and prevent the publication of radical political views. Or to defeat a pandemic, they might decide to close businesses and confine people to their homes. Unfortunately, there is no clear boundary between the legitimate protection of citizens' lives, property and security and the illegitimate oppression of citizens in the name of democratic government. All such proposals to curb rights, therefore, should be scrutinised and assessed with the most careful attention.

Peace and prosperity

It is often said that democracies do not take up arms against each other. This is not wholly true: on occasion they have done so. Yet there are many reasons why democratic systems may coexist more peacefully than other types of government. Electors are generally less enthusiastic about armed conflict than are military dictators; they have much to lose, after all, and a democratic government cannot simply ignore their lives, safety and property.

Arguably, liberal democracies are also more prosperous. Good government and prosperity have been in tandem over the last two centuries. But it is less clear that democracy *creates* more prosperity. Many countries, including the UK, became rich long before they had universal suffrage or made their elections fair and honest. So, it could not have been democracy that generated their wealth. If there is a single factor that promotes prosperity, it is arguably not democracy but *respect for individual rights*, such as allowing people to work, produce and trade on terms of their own choosing. But then democracies are more likely to respect those rights.

Though democracy is surprisingly robust, it has the potential to stall this liberal engine of freedom and prosperity. The moral force of having a majority at the polls may give governments the confidence to exploit wealth creators. That merely reduces the rewards of enterprise and discourages invention, investment and hard work, while encouraging idleness and consumption. This is hardly a recipe for prosperity.

Conclusion

Liberal democracy may well have real benefits over at least some other systems – especially its ability to adapt to change and to replace leaders and policies peacefully. It may promote better policy formation, protect individual rights, aid prosperity and encourage peace. But many of these supposed benefits are less clear than might be assumed. And democracy is not without its critics.

7 CRITICISMS OF DEMOCRACY

Democracy may have its benefits, but it also has its costs. It solves many problems, but it creates others. Critics argue that democracy is difficult to get right and easy to get wrong. Its performance record is not perfect. The rise of populist parties may be evidence that many electorates think democracy is serving them poorly. It is vulnerable to cronyism, bureaucracy, over-government, exploitation, the short-sightedness of voters (and of politicians who may be in office only a short time), and the erosion of individual rights. Does it really live up to its billing, in practice or even in principle?

Electors are not up to the job

One issue of principle is whether the electorate is a dependable foundation on which to build any system that can be trusted to take important decisions. The signs are not good: electors are very uninformed on political issues. That may be because they know that their single vote has almost no chance of determining the outcome of an election. It can be millions to one. So, there is no point in bothering to inform yourself on policy issues when your vote makes little or no difference.

Whatever the root cause, the depth of voter ignorance is startling. According to the American economist Bryan Caplan (2007) in *The Myth of the Rational Voter:*

> About half of Americans do not know that each state has two senators, and three-quarters do not know the length of their terms. About 70% cannot say which party controls the House and 60% which party controls the Senate. Over half cannot name their congressman, and 40% cannot name either of their senators ... Furthermore, these low knowledge levels have been stable since the dawn of polling, and international comparisons reveal Americans' overall political knowledge to be no more than moderately below average.

Nor do they always use their votes as democracy theorists suppose – that is, to choose the candidate they prefer. On the contrary, they may vote for other, sometimes radical candidates merely to send a message of discontent to their government, or even to give voice to their deeply held but ignorant, biased or prejudiced opinions. (It is said that when the twentieth-century American politician and diplomat Adlai Stevenson II was told by a supporter that he would get the votes of every thinking person in the US, he replied, 'I'm glad to hear it; but I need a majority!').

This tendency for electors to vote viscerally rather than rationally in turn prompts candidates to court these prejudices. In pursuit of popularity and votes, candidates for office (and elected politicians too) use slogans and sound-bites rather than considered and rational arguments. All of this, say democracy's critics, produces election results and public policy that is driven by bigotry and ignorance rather than evidence and reason.

Candidates and elected politicians also bend to the vested interests of lobbyists, who can muster large and committed voting blocks and whose support they rely on – in elections, in media campaigns and sometimes financially.

The potential rewards from lobbying can be very large. Succeed in getting a tax concession for your sector, or in imposing a regulation to keep out your competitors, or in landing a big government contract, and it can make an enormous difference to your business or your cause. Indeed, the potential rewards are so large that democratic government centres – like that within the 'Beltway' of highways around Washington, DC, or in the 'Village' that is London's Westminster area – are invariably populated thickly with lobbying firms and corporate public affairs offices.

But lobbying takes time, effort and money. (One Washington think tank puts the financial cost alone at around $3.5 billion per year.) The people who engage in lobbying are therefore generally those with some strong group or individual interest in changing public policy, or who are seeking special favours and treatment by the authorities. Their interests may be (and often are) very different from those of the wider public. All this makes lobbying a very costly, biased, unrepresentative and irrational way of influencing the policy decisions that the whole population will have to abide by; but, say critics, this is inherent in democracy itself.

The proposal of any new law or regulation ... ought always to be listened to with great precaution, and ought never to be adopted till after having been long and carefully examined, not only with the most scrupulous, but with the most suspicious attention. It comes from an order of men whose interest is never exactly the same with that of the public, who have generally an interest to deceive and even oppress the public, and who have, upon many occasions, both deceived and oppressed it.

— Adam Smith (1776), *The Wealth of Nations*,
Book I, Chapter XI

It makes inefficient decisions ...

Democracies are widely considered bad at taking difficult, controversial or urgent decisions. Because there are so many different views in play, among both the public and politicians, it can be hard to reach consensus and impossible to process the options quickly. National emergencies, demanding quick responses, are not the best time for lengthy parliamentary discussions. When powers are divided between different legislative chambers or between the legislature, executive and judiciary, it can take even longer to agree a policy.

Moreover, when issues are highly controversial, even if they are not urgent, the number of views that need to be reconciled can lead to long and intricate parliamentary and public debates. As the former UK Prime Minister Clement Attlee (1957) put it pithily: 'Democracy means government by discussion, but it is only effective if you can stop people talking'. And when opinion is evenly divided, or when there are many different possible options, the process might even produce deadlock. Often, things can only be resolved by 'horse trading' – making various, often irrelevant, concessions to different groups in order to buy their support – rather than on the basis of evidence and reason.

...and bad ones

There are many other reasons why democratically elected representative governments might make bad decisions. State power makes it easy for the majority to exploit others – particularly in terms of imposing taxes on them or confiscating their property. And when majority decisions are backed up by the power of the state and the supposed legitimacy of being 'democratic', there is no clear limit to how far this exploitation might go. At worst, it is legalised theft. At best, the threat of high taxes and confiscation discourages people from working hard and building up productive capital and wealth. It is also inefficient: people who spend their own earnings, say critics, probably spend them more carefully and cost-effectively than politicians who spend money that they force out of taxpayers.

Even worse, by appealing to voters' prejudices, politicians often make decisions that are clearly harmful. Nearly all economists agree on the merits of free trade, for instance; but politicians, pandering to producers' and the public's concerns about foreign competition, commonly endorse protectionist policies such as import quotas and tariffs instead. To them, the immediate threat of voters complaining about 'foreigners taking our jobs' outweighs the more distant and dispersed prosperity promised by trade liberalisation.

It has a short-term focus

Bad decision-making is encouraged by the fact that elected leaders' careers are short. They enjoy the short-term praise for popular policies, but they are rarely still in office long enough to be held accountable for any longer-term damage that these policies create. It therefore makes political sense for them to borrow or print more money in order to boost their spending, while leaving their successors to deal with the resulting public debt or inflation.

A more rational system of government, say critics, would produce policies that aimed for and created long-term prosperity for its citizens – not policies driven by the short-term desire of politicians to be loved. A rational system would not allow productive people to be taxed and exploited merely to appease the envy of the majority or the majority's desire for free benefits at the expense of others. But without strict limits being imposed, 'democratic' systems do precisely that. Instead of helping to build up investment for the future, they steal and spend capital for consumption today. Inevitably, this damages the long-term prosperity of the whole society.

And since almost everyone is involved in this process as voters, they are told that it is 'their' government and its decisions are 'their' decisions. Such language suggests that the bullying or robbing of minority groups by the majority is normal, legitimate, and no longer immoral – as it would be if any other group did it.

It rests on state power

However bad an elected government's decisions might be, you cannot escape them. Majority decisions are imposed even on those who disagree with them, through the threat of fines, imprisonment, the revocation of licences and trade permits, and many other sanctions. Nor is there any escape: ordinary citizens are denied the right to use force against anyone, including a government that exploits them.

It is true that democratic decision-making helps solve the 'free rider' problem. Everyone benefits from public services such as defence and policing, so it seems fair to require everyone to contribute to their cost. The trouble, say critics, is that once we concede the principle that the state can take people's money, there is no logical stopping point.

Similarly, it may also be thought reasonable that a government should be able to curb individual and civil rights in times of emergency – spying on or even detaining people who are suspected of planning terrorism, for example. But, say critics, when the state is given 'emergency' powers there is likewise no clear boundary on their use. And as F. A. Hayek (1979) noted, 'Emergencies have always been the pretext on which the safeguards of individual liberty have been eroded...'.

For example, the 2007–8 financial crisis led to Western governments taking over banks and imposing heavy regulation on other financial businesses. Just over a decade later, during the Covid-19 pandemic, even the most liberal of liberal democracies imposed astonishing restrictions on people's movements (including confining them at home), as well as closing businesses (such as gyms, sporting events, hairdressers and restaurants), banning the sale of 'non-essential' goods, and massively expanding the state sector. In early 2020, many people were willing to accept such restrictions voluntarily, in the interest of controlling the virus. But as the year went on and the restrictions continued (or even deepened), public resentment against them grew. Politicians then found themselves using state powers to impose controls on a significant number of unwilling citizens who complained that they were now living in a 'police state'.

If individual rights can be suspended so easily in the world's most liberal democracies, critics argue, we are right to be wary of the powers that an election majority bestows on our political leaders. Whatever powers we grant them can also be used against us – deliberately or unwittingly. Politicians may not understand the vital long-term importance of strong protections on rights, nor even realise that they are violating them. And even if they do realise, they still face powerful short-term incentives to maximise their own authority.

Despite all that, as we have seen, democracies have proved remarkably stable. The historical periods where liberal values have prevailed in government are arguably those when civilisation advanced most quickly – not just economically but in science, technology, art, education, literature and much else. Nobody would willingly sacrifice such progress. The main worry is that we erode it by mistake.

It promotes over-large government

Supporters of democracy believe that it is politically neutral – working equally well for populations who favour small government and for those who favour more social and economic intervention. But again, democracy is designed specifically for *collective* decision-making – a point not lost on Marxists like the Polish theorist Rosa Luxemburg (1899) when she wrote candidly, 'Democracy is indispensable to socialism'.

Though liberals try to set limits on the scope of government, there remains no objective way to decide exactly which decisions should be made collectively, and which should be left to individuals. And, in practice, democracy seems far from politically neutral. In the early 1900s, democratic governments rarely took more than 10 per cent of national income; by the early 2000s, 40–50 per cent had become quite normal – reflecting the volume of decisions that are now made collectively and no longer by individuals.

Over the course of the twentieth century, collective provision came to dominate vast areas of life – from welfare to healthcare, housing, education, insurance, transport, utilities, manufacturing and much else. Perhaps such expansion was given legitimacy by the widening of the franchise, particularly to women. And as government budgets enlarged as a result of two world wars, more and more interest groups sought more and more favours from the state – which politicians, in their quest for votes, granted.

The same forces persist today. The vote motive of politicians, and the supposed wisdom and legitimacy of majority voting, prompts even 'liberal', 'conservative' or 'free market' parties to expand collective decision-making more and more deeply into more and more areas of economic, social and individual life. Politicians also vie for attention and votes by promoting large, impressive but often costly and wasteful public projects, often on borrowed money, rather than urging sound financial management. 'Our form of democracy is bribery, on the highest scale', as the American writer Gore Vidal put it in *Armageddon* (1987). And all this can produce a government that is bigger than most people really want.

It has unseen costs

While the benefits of democratic systems are easily appreciated, their financial, social and moral costs are often overlooked. Far from encouraging social harmony, say critics, democracy actually promotes bad behaviour – with political parties fighting like gangs for attention and supremacy, politicians focusing on the next election rather than the long-term health of the nation, and lobby groups cynically using the system to get special treatment at other peoples' expense.

So, continue the critics, it is no surprise that democracy has given us larger, costlier and more centralised government over the last century. Politicians, businesses and other interest groups all have an interest in expanding the state sector and squeezing more power or favours from it. As different groups vote themselves more benefits and pass the costs on to others, including future generations, who have no power to resist, taxes and debt creep ever upwards.

> A democracy is a place where numerous elections are held, at great cost, without issues, and with interchangeable candidates.
> — Gore Vidal (1991), *A View from the Diner's Club*

It is not easy to neuter these forces or displace the political class that controls them. Politics has *high entry barriers*, as economists say: it is hard for newer and smaller parties to break into government, particularly in 'first past the post' voting systems. So, there is rarely significant challenge to the prevailing cronyism. But the rise of populist movements might indicate that this is changing.

8   OVER-SELLING DEMOCRACY?

'Democracy' has achieved almost mythical status as the bringer of peace, prosperity, fairness and freedom. That is why leaders are so keen to apply the word to their own governments, even if in reality they are autocracies. It is also why people who live in liberal democracies often overstate democracy's capabilities. We need to look through the exaggerations and see how far the reality measures up.

Democracy is the best system

It is often said that democracy is the best political system – or, at any rate, the least bad. Unfortunately, we would need to try all other imaginable systems in order to know that for sure. And even then, by what standards should we judge a political system? Democracy is good at involving citizens in public affairs, for example, but it can be slow and indecisive during crises. It can be corrupt, but it seems better than most in terms of promoting human welfare, prosperity and freedom. Indeed, a survey by the American economists Robert Lawson, Ryan Murphy and Benjamin Powell (2020) found that democracy is strongly associated with economic freedom. But whether it should be judged overall as 'the best' system remains a question of personal judgement.

> No one pretends that democracy is perfect or all-wise. Indeed, it has been said that democracy is the worst form of government except all those other forms that have been tried from time to time.
> — Sir Winston Churchill (1947), *Hansard*, November 11

It's rule by the people

Democracy is often called 'rule by the people'. That is wrong. In modern democracies, the people do not rule; they choose their rulers. They do not decide the laws; their representatives decide them.

Furthermore, 'the people' are not a single decision maker, but millions of individuals with different – and often competing – views on public affairs. They disagree on what the ends of public policy should be, as well as on how to achieve those ends. They cannot and do not agree on how to 'rule'. Democracy does not produce some noble and enduring consensus: what prevails is the opinion of whichever group can muster more votes than others. Critics say that this process is not 'rule by the people' but more like gang warfare.

It's government by consent

Democracy is said to be 'government by consent'. To some extent this is true. But critics argue that the reality of democracy is that legislative decisions are made by political elites. The only 'consent' from the public is the scant consent given by the majority of individuals who bother to vote in elections that are usually many years apart.

Moreover, you cannot be said to 'consent' if other people make the decisions for you. But that is what happens in democracy. The majority decide the policy, and everyone else has to accept that or face sanctions such as fines or imprisonment. Even if you vote against them, the majority still dominate your life and raid your purse just like any autocrat.

Nor is the supposed 'consent' of voters even rational and informed. Not only are they ignorant about the detailed issues. No voter can forecast the future either. So, they cannot predict exactly how candidates will perform, nor foresee the wider effects (good or bad) of their policies. In other words, say critics, their votes have no rational basis at all.

Bryan Caplan (2007) argues that things are even worse. Voters, he says, are *systematically* prejudiced and irrational. They think things are getting worse when they are not; they believe that creating jobs is more important than creating value; they are biased against foreigners and in favour of protecting domestic industries; and they are swayed excessively by recent but irrelevant events, such as their country's Olympic medal performance. All these biases lead to policy decisions that are *systematically* irrational, distorted and damaging.

Everyone has a say

It is claimed that democracy 'gives everyone an equal say' on public policy. But not 'everyone' is allowed to vote. For much of history, even the most liberal nations denied votes to women, as well as those without property and ethnic minorities. And electors who *choose* not to vote – often half or more of the population – have no say in the result at all. But then, even if you do vote, the chance of your vote actually deciding the outcome of an election in a large country is tens (or even hundreds) of millions to one.

> Democracy is the theory that the common people know what they want and deserve to get it good and hard.
> — H. L. Mencken (1915), *A Few Pages of Notes*

Nor do people's votes count equally. The votes of people living in a 'safe' electoral district – one where the same party always wins – count for much less than those of people in a 'marginal' area. And for practical demographic reasons, some voting districts may have far more electors than others. So, if each district elects just one representative, the votes of those who live in smaller ones have much more weight.

But representation may be manipulated for political reasons too. For example, the early Soviet Union gave five times more representation to urban dwellers, in a deliberate effort to overcome rural conservatism. American politicians too had a long history of creating oddly shaped electoral districts in order to keep them 'safe' for incumbent colleagues. (The map of one such district, created in 1812 under Massachusetts Governor Elbridge Gerry, came to look like a salamander – giving us the term 'gerrymander'.)

Democracy promotes equality

Democratic systems are often hailed for asserting the political (or 'civic') equality, and the dignity, of individuals. But other systems may have political equality too; and we can still respect people's dignity, even if we do not let them vote.

It is also claimed that democratic participation promotes self-esteem and self-expression. But it would be odd to construct a voting system specifically for these purposes. We might not want to give the vote to sociopathic prisoners in the mere hope of raising their self-esteem, for example. And there are far better ways of promoting self-esteem and self-expression than elections.

Similarly, democracy is said to produce fairness and equality, and prevent the political and social dominance of small cliques. Yet there is every reason to believe that better-off groups still have disproportionate influence. Senior ministers and government officials tend to be wealthier than the average, and there are more graduates from expensive schools and universities in their ranks. Also, the articulate middle classes actually seem to benefit more than the poor from state services, such as pensions, schools and healthcare; but then they dominate the political debate, which helps them secure political decisions in their favour. Their influence may be one reason why, in many countries, the state sector has grown so large – much larger than would be needed if its sole purpose were to provide cash and services to the relatively few people who actually depend on them.

Democracy provides a sense of community

Another argument is that democracy delivers a 'sense of community' and produces 'harmony'. But a sense of community or belonging is more likely to come from people's participation in clubs, charities, churches, support groups and all the other institutions of *civil society*. And while elected representative government certainly helps in making collective decisions peacefully, it hardly produces harmony. Elections and legislative debates are contests between different and opposing interest groups. They can get very bitter, since the winners have the power to impose their view on the losers.

In economic markets, people choose goods and services for themselves, not for other people. Different people can make whatever personal choices they like – Apple or Android, tea or coffee, red or blue – and their choices make no difference to others. Political choices, however, are made for everyone. When the majority vote for a particular set of candidates, everyone has to accept the result. When the ruling party decides on a policy – to build a new road or airport, say – everyone has to accept it, including those whose homes and livelihoods will be demolished in the process.

The binding nature of political decisions, and the fact that majorities can make wide-ranging decisions about so many things, means that other people's choices can have a profound effect on your own life and welfare. As the American philosopher Jason Brennan (2016) notes in *Against Democracy*, politics turns your neighbours into potential enemies, rather than friends. This is the very opposite of 'a sense of community'.

Democracy protects us from bad rulers

For most of human history, our lives have been ruled by autocrats – warlords, monarchs, tsars, emperors, chiefs, aristocrats, lairds, protectors, dictators and others. Often, these rulers had the power of life and death over us. Certainly, democratic systems may make it harder for leaders to accumulate power or use power viciously and arbitrarily. But politicians and officials still have their own personal interests – raising their own status and salaries, for example, or diverting public funds to their supporters. The democratic process gives them the power and apparent legitimacy to indulge those interests, even if other people's interests are damaged in the process. It might even attract bad rulers, rather than save us from them.

Nor can we always rely on democracy's provision of justice to save us. It might spare us from the worst and most arbitrary actions by our leaders. But like all monopolies, it can be slow and expensive. And insofar as it is part of the state, justice can be twisted to serve the interests of those in command of state authority. Ultimately, the surest safeguard of our lives, property, freedom of expression and other basic rights is not democracy or the courts, but a general public appreciation of liberal values. If our rights are to survive and democracy is to deliver its optimum benefits to us all, it is essential that liberals and democrats explain those values and promote their general appreciation by the public. And we must remain keenly aware of the fault lines that exist within the democratic decision-making process itself.

9 HOW DEMOCRATIC DECISIONS ARE MADE

The nineteenth-century German Chancellor Otto von Bismarck supposedly once commented that if you like laws or sausages, you should never watch either being made. And there are indeed good reasons to be queasy about the way that democracies decide things. Democracy is supposed to translate the opinions of many individuals into a single set of collective decisions. But we need to be aware of where, how and why this process might be less than perfect.

Elections

Elections, for example, have obvious limitations as methods of choosing between candidates or policies. For a start, they are infrequent – sometimes only every four, five, or more years. (In the commercial marketplace, by contrast, we can choose our preferred products any hour of any day.) The choice that elections offer to voters is also very limited. A large number of diverse and complex public issues are put to voters as packages, presented by perhaps only two or three candidates. (Again, the marketplace offers us choices between vast ranges of individual products, not just a few packages.) Then, the majority's decisions are imposed on everyone.

There is also the 'rock, paper, scissors' paradox. Voters may prefer one candidate over a second (like paper over rock) and that second candidate over a third (like rock over scissors); but then they might well prefer the third (scissors) over the first (paper). Because of this, the order in which votes are taken can make a huge difference to the outcome. In France and other countries where the leading candidates from an initial voting round go into a final run-off, for instance, it is common for a candidate to lead the field in the first round but be roundly defeated in the binary choice presented in the second.

Electors

Electors have a whole range of different motives. They may be lifetime supporters of one particular party, whatever the issues. They may simply want to cause the ruling party discomfort. Or they may vote solely on some local or personal concern, such as the closure of a nearby hospital. They may not even vote for what they really want, but vote tactically, for a candidate they dislike, in order to keep out another that they dislike even more. Or they may be completely confused about the issues but still feel a duty to vote. (A surprising number do not make up their minds until they are in the voting booth with the ballot paper before them.)

Elections are not ideal, rational processes in which thoughtful, informed, detached electors carefully ponder the issues of the day and vote for what they consider best for the long-term good of the country as a whole.

Candidates

Even the most public-spirited politician has to gather votes to reach office and achieve anything at all. This 'vote motive' is therefore a big driver for them, which again distorts the decision-making process.

For example, politicians tend to focus on 'median' voters. After all, there are far more electors in the political centre than on the extremes, and they are more likely to be persuaded to change their minds than those on the extremes. But when candidates and parties all pitch themselves to the centre, it denies voters a real choice – particularly those with strong but non-centrist views.

Politicians are also strongly focused on lobby groups, who can deliver them large numbers of votes because of their strong motivation and organisation – particularly when they team up with yet other interest groups. It is the 'silent majority' who will end up footing the bill – but the 'silent majority' have little voice.

Legislators

The representatives chosen by this process, therefore, are by no means detached guardians of the public interest. They are compromised even before they take their seat. They have promises to keep to the interest groups that supported them and the bosses of the political party that gave them their election branding.

Getting their policies through the legislature is an unprincipled process too. It may require them to engage in *logrolling*: a 'you vote for my policy and I'll vote for yours' exchange. For example, one representative may vote for another's proposal to have a new school or hospital built in their district, not because of any belief in its merits, but in the hope that the other will return the favour in the future.

Likewise, larger legislative initiatives may need to be packaged to gain the necessary support. Thus, in the early 1950s, the US President Dwight D. Eisenhower designed his interstate highway plans so that they benefited a majority of states. In voting for better roads for their own state, senators and representatives found themselves voting for the whole network, whether or not they thought it a good idea. And the 2008 emergency 'TARP' Bill to bail out troubled US banks started just two pages long when presented to Congress. But since everyone knew that the Bill simply *had* to pass, Representatives demanded all sorts of favours in return for their support. The Bill ended up at 451 pages, full of concessions such as tax breaks for fabric producers, distillers, fishing fleets, motorsports complexes and even makers of wooden arrows.

Professional politicians and interested bureaucrats react to the incentives provided by lobbyists and pressure groups to push a relentless growth in government activity. When, in living memory, has there been a significant process of repealing legislation?

> — Craig Smith and Tom Miers (2011),
> *Democracy and the Fall of the West*

Officials

The officials charged with putting all this legislation into place are not selfless angels either. They may take pride in working for the public, but they still have their own personal interests. For example, if they can expand their own agency, then their budgets, salaries, status, job security and promotion prospects may all improve.

And they can serve their own interests in other ways. For example, laws are broad in their effect, and often need officials such as regulators to decide what the precise rules should be and how those rules should be interpreted and administered. Being experts in their own governmental area (probably more so than the politicians passing the legislation), officials can easily add complexity to the law – which then requires more officials to administer it.

They can also leave themselves a great deal of discretion over how the laws operate. That in turn gives them status and self-importance because it makes businesses and the public dependent on their interpretation of the rules or on their ability to decide who should get contracts, grants or licences. They might sometimes even be able to extract bribes or favours for their decisions.

Political dependents

The media, lobby groups, think tanks, and those who depend on government spending all have an interest in preserving and expanding the collective decision-making process.

Broadcasters, for example, need to fill their demanding 24-hour news cycles. Luckily for them, politicians are desperate to air their views and 'spin' their policies. The media also want 'scoops' – and again, government politicians oblige them, by 'leaking' policies in advance of any official announcement, so that the public get to hear their side of the case before their opponents even know what is happening.

Think tanks and campaign groups might present themselves as experts and claim to be detached, but they too bring their own interests into the debate. Campaign groups, highly focused on some key issue, are likely to call for more public spending or tax reliefs for it, without thinking much about the impact of this on taxpayers more generally.

Lastly, there are individuals who are dependent on the state. Government employees are a large voting group, one that is unlikely to vote for smaller government and less bureaucracy. But there are millions of others, such as pensioners, welfare beneficiaries, and those who supply government bodies. In some advanced countries, the number of people who rely on the state for half or more of their income is a majority of the population. Their interest is to expand the state; not to save taxpayers' money.

Conclusion

Democracy is better in many ways than other, more autocratic systems of government, but we should not get misty-eyed about it. When we talk about 'democracy' and democratic decision-making, we are really talking about politics and political decision-making. And as most people will agree, the political process is far from perfect.

To secure the greatest benefits from democracy, therefore, we must remain realistic about how it actually works. We should be alert to its fault lines and, where possible, try to correct or mitigate those faults. If we succeed, the rewards can be considerable.

10 DEMOCRACY UNDER PRESSURE

Though almost everyone claims to love the idea of democracy, many people have become far more sceptical about its actual workings. They love democracy but hate politics. They see democracy as a fair way to involve everyone, and openly debate public issues, leading to a considered, fair and peaceful execution of agreed policies. But they see politics and politicians as duplicitous, self-serving and self-interested. In polls of public trust in different professions, politicians invariably come at or near the bottom.

This is not all the fault of politicians themselves. It is not easy for them to translate the diverse views of millions of people into a single policy that everyone can support. That is even harder today, when travel and migration have made many populations more diverse. Politicians also have strong but opposing views, leading to big arguments – making the public think they are more interested in point-scoring than principle. To reach agreement at all, they often have to compromise – making them look even more unprincipled.

Nor is it something unique to democracy or something that is worse in democracies. On the contrary, democracy can promote honesty and openness in public debate.

Politicians in relatively liberal democracies may in general be more honest and less corrupt than those in other systems. For example, of the fifteen countries perceived as being the least corrupt, as measured by the Berlin-based NGO Transparency International (2019), fourteen are rated as 'full democracies' by the Economist Intelligence Unit (2019). (The exception is Singapore, which is rated as a 'flawed democracy'.)

Rejection of establishment politics

In other words, politicians in democracies may be relatively blameless; but then in democracies, their actions are more visible to the public and more open to public criticism. That in turn may be why they are indeed more criticised.

In many countries, the public criticism of politics has led to declining turnouts at elections and rising support for so-called (and sometimes extreme) populist movements and parties – which in turn are happy to exploit this frustration with mainstream politicians. Populist leaders regard themselves as the true democrats, defending the interests of the ordinary but unrepresented mass of the people. They may gloss over the complexities of issues such as immigration or welfare – but then the public have little time for such complexities anyway.

Changing world circumstances

Economic crises have also fuelled the public disillusionment with democratic politics. Liberal democracy is commonly associated with economic growth: as Acemoglu and Robinson (2012) found, economic success comes through having the right economic and political institutions. But the West's economic slowdown after the financial crisis of 2007–8, the economic disruption of the 2020 Covid pandemic, and the apparent inability of politicians to handle these crises, may have undermined public faith in democracy.

Another possible source of disillusionment is that some global issues have grown beyond the abilities of national politics to control or decide. Climate change is one: people complain that voting to reduce carbon emissions in their own country is pointless unless other countries do the same. Security, terrorism and migration may also need coordinated international solutions.

International bodies try to fill the vacuum on these global issues – the EU leading on environmental policy, central banks trying to coordinate economic stability, and international courts, for example. But such agencies have severe limitations. They lack a cultural and linguistic identity that voters might empathise with, and their constituent nations may disagree strongly on both aims and methods. People therefore regard these bodies as distant and unaccountable, and call for more national assertiveness instead – something which populist leaders are again very happy to exploit.

Changes in the political system

Another challenge is that the rising volume and complexity of the decisions now made through the political process has made politics an activity for professional politicians. Ordinary citizens often feel they have little role. Very few do more than vote. Only a tiny minority join parties or campaign groups. As parties have lost members, they have become more reliant on slick marketing, personalities, soundbites and spin – which just makes electors suspect that they are being lied to.

Modern media technology might make politicians more visible, but its attention is focused mostly on party leaders rather than ordinary parliamentarians. It is ministers and prime ministers who appear on TV debates, boosting their status and authority and consolidating their control over their parties. That shifts power to the executive and away from the representatives who are supposed to restrain them.

Meanwhile the rising cost of elections makes money more important, leading the public to question who is funding their politics. They vote out politicians, only to see them stepping into some well-paid role in a company that wants to exploit their inside knowledge of the political and regulatory system. It all fuels the idea that politicians are in it only for themselves. Again, this is not something unique to democracy; it is simply more visible under it.

The growth and complexity of government also mean that more and more decisions are taken by officials and 'experts' rather than by elected representatives. Politicians scarcely have time to read and understand all the complex legislation that is put to them. In fact, many of the laws passed in modern democracies are drafted by civil servants and are so complex that they need yet other experts to interpret them and agencies to enforce them. So, politicians are again eclipsed. And many of the expert panels set up to review legislation are chosen from an elite of academics, judges or civil servants who are even more distant from the public than the politicians themselves.

Changes in the electorate

The electorate has changed too. With increasing wealth, wider education and easier travel, class and caste barriers have broken down. It is easier for people from poor families to use their talent, to become rich and even famous, and shake up the given economic and political norms. But then people in the declining industries come to feel undervalued and excluded, again encouraging nationalism and populism.

Technology has changed politics too. For example, more people now get their news from online sources. Social media makes it easier for minorities to find like-minded others – and to support each other, without needing politicians. And many services (for example, broadcasting, utilities, telephones and transport) that once could only be delivered by large public agencies controlled by politicians can now be delivered in diverse new ways by smaller, competing private firms. Not only does that make politicians less relevant to people who use these services; it also makes people wonder why they cannot have the same choice in public services such as schools or pensions, rather than have politicians decide for them.

Changing age profiles – the baby boomer generation in the West and the rising number of millennials elsewhere – has also affected attitudes. Young people complain that the older generation that dominate politics have used their political power to skew things in their own favour. Thus, the older generation have voted themselves generous benefits such as pensions, social insurance and free healthcare, partly financed by debt that they are leaving the younger generation to pay off. It is another source of disillusionment with the normal political process.

Conclusion

For all these reasons, the public have become increasingly alienated from their democratic politicians. Hence the rise of fringe parties. The worry for those who support democracy is that public contempt for the current political class could expand into a wider loss of faith in the democratic process itself. This could be a serious misfortune, given the considerable benefits of liberal democracy. So, it is important that we understand the source of the current disillusionment and seek ways to make democratic politics more relevant to the public.

11 THE FUTURE OF PARTICIPATION

Forms of participation

Some people think that democracy's woes can be cured by new forms of public participation. Their ideal is a 'participative' democracy, more like democracy in its old meaning, with citizens directly involved in decision making. They contrast this against today's 'aggregative' methods, which merely count people's votes and balance them off.

Compulsory voting is one suggestion. It is only weakly 'participative' in that nobody has to do more than vote, but the hope is that it also stimulates wider interest in the public debate. A number of countries already have compulsory voting, famously Australia but also other democracies such as Uruguay, Belgium and Luxembourg. Yet there is little evidence that it has any effect on election results or the quality of public debate.

Another suggestion is *direct democracy* such as referendums and ballot initiatives, which gives everyone a direct vote on legislation. Again, this is already used in various places. Some US states also have 'veto' referendums that allow voters to block the introduction of unpopular laws. California allows citizens to propose laws and even amendments to the State Constitution.

A third strategy is *deliberative polling*. A representative sample of the population are polled for their opinions. Then, they are invited together for a weekend to discuss the findings. They are provided with briefings on the arguments. They discuss the issues between themselves and with experts and politicians. They are then polled again, to see what difference informed discussion has on the original poll findings. This, it is said, helps legislators to understand the public's real values more accurately.

A variant of this is *citizens' juries*, where a small but representative group, normally 12–24 people, meet together, question expert witnesses, and deliberate on the issues. The idea is that their findings then influence the wider public's choices, and those of legislators.

Many people have advocated *digital democracy*. Around two-thirds of people who do not vote at the ballot box say that they would vote online if they could do so. Advocates of this idea point out that online systems allow voters to be given more detailed information about the issues and the arguments before they make their decision.

Information technology is already shaping the democratic process. Australia has pioneered the 'MiVote' platform, which gives electors a variety of perspectives on all major issues being debated in Parliament. Iceland in 2008 'crowdsourced' its constitutional reforms. Estonia calls itself an 'e-nation'. And machine learning and translation systems now make it possible to have large-scale debates involving people across the globe.

But does technology really boost informed public debate? The evidence suggests not: while it gives people access to vast amounts of information and enables them to vote on a wide range of issues (not just the selection of candidates for office), they remain rationally ignorant because their time is scarce, and their individual votes still count for little.

Arguments for participation

One answer to that might be to involve people more in the decision-making process. And there are other arguments for this as well. Many people regard involving citizens in social decisions as good in itself. It gets people thinking about the issues. It boosts their social awareness. By making them better informed, it should lead to better choices. And it can be done at all levels – governments can harness the wisdom of the whole country on important national questions, while the tenants in a single housing block could use the same idea to decide on how their building is run.

There are practical arguments too. Old-style voting methods make democracy over-centralised, cumbersome, slow and limited in scope. Politicians cannot possibly take everyone's views into account, leading to policy that works well for some but badly for others. More decentralised decision-making is faster and produces policies that are more relevant to local people and are therefore more stable. While old-style politics can only bombard voters *en masse* with slogans and soundbites, online systems give them access to whole websites of relevant information. And this sort of participative democracy can break the control of the established parties, allowing new ideas to flourish and changing social conditions to be acted on more quickly.

Practical arguments against participation

Critics remain unconvinced. They argue that direct democracy techniques such as referendums or ballot initiatives still require voters to invest precious time and effort in learning about and deliberating on the issues, even though their individual vote still carries miniscule weight. And if we cannot rely on electors to make informed decisions, it is probably better to leave governing to their better-informed representatives. 'Democracy is not a state in which the people, continually assembled, itself directs public affairs', wrote the French revolutionary leader Maximilien Robespierre (1794). 'Democracy is a state in which the people, as sovereign ... does for itself what it can do well and does what it cannot through its delegates...'.

Furthermore, US experience suggests that *ballot initiatives* will be largely driven by the established political parties, since they have the greatest funding and campaigning capacity. Also, ballot initiatives are often ill-designed or promoted by interest groups which seek to exploit taxpayers or do down rival interests – meaning that every election sees businesses wasting millions of dollars to fight off malicious or inept proposals. And the system produces financially and legally inconsistent decisions.

Referendums seem at odds with representative democracy – the whole point of which is to spare electors having to decide every issue by delegating the task to their representatives. So, what do referendums exist for? Can they make law (in which case some very inconsistent and illiberal laws are likely to be passed)? Do they direct representatives how to vote (and what happens if representatives vote the other way)? Or are they merely advisory (in which case, why not simply rely on the opinion polls)? There are often no clear answers to these questions. But even though the exact role of referendums within representative democracy may be unclear, they may well have a positive function. Evidence compiled by the American academic John G. Matsusaka (2004) strongly suggests that local referendums can and do help resolve political disputes and save taxpayers money.

As for *digital democracy*, critics say that it will still be driven by established parties and well-funded lobby groups. And some citizens, particularly older people, may have less access to online participation, undermining the concept of political equality.

Regarding *deliberative* systems, critics such as Jason Brennan (2016) argue that they make *worse* decisions than conventional aggregative methods. Deliberative groups tend to amplify received wisdom, not explore new ideas. Participants are easily led by forceful individuals with strong views. In theory, independent facilitators should be able to correct for this; but inevitably facilitators are likely to bring their own prejudices into the discussion. On the other hand, some people with unfashionable views may be embarrassed to state them in front of strangers – though fully willing to express them anonymously in the ballot booth. So again, deliberative groups will tend to come up with conventional and centrist conclusions that do not represent the full spread of public opinion.

Against participation in principle

The critics also argue that participation through formal channels is no more 'democratic' than what already exists. Citizens already communicate directly, and in large numbers, through social and other media, a form of participation that is much more immediate and extensive than any citizens' jury could be. And it is not clear that more formal participation methods do actually help educate and enlighten the electorate. Compulsory voting, for example, does not seem to increase citizens' knowledge on political issues, or change election outcomes.

In any case, the critics continue, the problem is not education but *motivation*. Electors are bombarded with information every day; they simply ignore it because they have more pressing personal business to worry about. And people differ greatly in terms of their desire to be involved anyway. Only a few join parties, deliver leaflets, attend political meetings or donate money to causes. So why should we assume that everyone would want to deliberate on public issues if they were offered the chance? Most could imagine nothing duller.

Participation through formal arrangements, conclude its critics, is simply not useful to most people. They will not value it, respect it, or use the opportunity wisely. It is not intrinsically better or more 'democratic' than what we already have.

Do we really want 'more democracy'?

There are other strong reasons, says Brennan (2016), why greater 'participative' democracy might actually produce worse results. We know that voters are shockingly ignorant about public affairs; the idea that participation can somehow turn them into policy experts is absurd. They probably cannot even be made into competent amateurs – and would resent the attempt to do so. Other things such as work, home, family and hobbies are more urgent or important to them. Making them engage in politics is therefore positively harmful to them: it diverts their time from things they value and want to do, into something they do not.

And should politics be such a large part of our lives anyway? It does not seem to make people more socially aware or more moral; it may be more likely to corrupt them. The lure of political power is tempting, as is the prospect of imposing your own views on the lives of others. The whole point of liberal democracy is to limit such power and so prevent those in authority bullying and exploiting others. But the more that collective decision-making is given legitimacy by calling it 'participative democracy', the easier that becomes, and the harder it is for minorities to resist.

Why, then, are so many political activists so keen on 'more' or 'deeper' democracy? Perhaps they truly believe that it would boost important values such as political equality, or be more transparent, or morally uplifting, or take power from the political insiders. But there may be less charitable explanations. Perhaps they simply want to legitimise and expand collective decision-making, thinking it a better way to run a society than leaving decisions to individuals. Perhaps they recognise that voters tend to be more interventionist than their elected representatives. Or perhaps they think a more interventionist government will provide more jobs and status for intellectuals like themselves.

The idea of limited democracy

If voters are indeed irrational, uninformed, tribal and self-interested, the real question is not how to change them (which seems a forlorn hope), but why they should have any power over other people at all. It is an argument, not for *more* democracy, but for *more limited* democracy – for a restrained government that does not usurp the decisions that we can make for ourselves but focuses on its key role of protecting our rights, freedoms and security.

The liberal view of democracy is that we created it to protect us, not to control us. It is not a mechanism for allowing majorities to run large portions of everyone's lives. It is merely a way of choosing representatives who might be better informed, more interested and more capable to make those few decisions that have to be made jointly. Rather than trying to make electors something they have no wish to be, it might be better to build institutions so as to create the best government possible on the basis of voters as they actually are.

12 DEMOCRACY AND BORDERS

The fall of the Berlin Wall in 1989 put autocratic government on the defensive. The grim reality of the Soviet Union was exposed, and authoritarian regimes in general began to lose their legitimacy. Democracy of some sort seemed to be the only alternative. Reform movements spread through Eastern Europe, Latin America, Africa (notably with the end of apartheid in 1994), South Asia, South East Asia, even for a time in China. More and more countries became designated as 'free' on the international indexes.

The American political scientist Francis Fukuyama (1992) even talked of 'the end of history' – a world in which liberal democracy had triumphed everywhere. Western politicians considered it their duty to make that vision come true by spreading democracy round the globe. Dictators were challenged. Foreign aid and trade deals were made conditional on countries ending corruption, reforming their governments and adopting democratic institutions.

Liberal democracy is not, however, so easy to create or reproduce. As the US Supreme Court Justice Anthony Kennedy (1999) observed: 'Democracy is something that you must learn each generation. It has to be taught'. And indeed, it took some of the first modern democracies centuries of conflict and bloodshed to learn. Today, with many working examples of democracy now in existence, new democracies can perhaps be established more quickly and peacefully.

Yet obstacles remain. In order to work and deliver its benefits, democracy needs citizens who accept it, understand it, value it and respect it. But people who have always lived under autocratic government often fear and misunderstand democracy. Sometimes, dictators such as Egypt's Hosni Mubarak and those of other Middle Eastern and North African states have been replaced by 'democratic' regimes that in some ways are even less liberal because the revolutionaries who are voted into office imagine that their majority gives them absolute power. By adopting the trappings of democracy, even though they abuse its principles, they claim an international legitimacy that is undeserved. In other places, dictators such as Josip Tito in Yugoslavia managed to suppress conflict between nationalist, religious or ethnic groups in their country, only for deeply destructive warfare to break out once they were removed. It seems that people's fears about transitioning from autocracy to democracy have some justification.

The West's mistakes

Democracy cannot simply be planted in new soil and be expected to flourish on its own. It requires cultivation and care. Nor can democracy automatically deliver prosperity, rights, freedom and equality to countries where these things are unknown and foreign. Sadly, Western politicians believed they could achieve all that and more. And because they thought that democracy produces freedom and prosperity (when in reality, it is liberal values that produce these things), they thought that poorer countries, once free of dictatorship, would eagerly create their own democratic institutions.

But Westerners have lived with liberal and democratic institutions for so long that they take them for granted. They assume that justice, the rule of law, rights, trust and honesty exist everywhere – or will instantly spring back to life once repression is lifted. They assume that all countries have a common sense of nationhood, and an educated, liberal middle class who will understand and drive democratic reforms.

Yet countries that have lived under autocracy for centuries may have none of these things, nor any clear concept of them. There may be deep hatred and little trust between ethnic or other groups. People may believe that a country cannot operate without strong autocratic leadership. They may regard the established democracies as weak, bloated and discordant. They may continue to value stability over freedom, tradition over prosperity, religion over law.

Ryan Murphy (2018) has shown that, taking all other factors into account, autocracy does not in fact lead to better governance outcomes. But convincing the world of the benefits of democracy may not be so easy.

Problems of emergent democracies

Indeed, when countries do adopt the trappings of democracy – elections, parliaments, courts – they still may not adopt the reality. There may be no rule of law. The courts may be corrupt. Rights may be insecure or restricted to the few. Religious conformity may stifle individual freedom. Elections may be a sham, with no real choice of candidates and votes not fairly counted. Parliament may be dominated by a single party. Election victors may use their 'democratic mandate' to persecute opponents.

And there may be no common feeling of nationhood at all. Ethnic, tribal, cultural, ideological or religious conflicts may have created lasting bitterness and disunity. Feuding political parties may produce a weak and dysfunctional state. Sometimes the only people with any authority and respect are opposing warlords. People may see military power as the only way to stabilise things; or as necessary to impose their religious or political ideology on others.

A strong military government, therefore, may well gain more popularity than any idea of a free, democratic one. At the same time, religious and political zealots may regard their opponents as wicked beyond redemption, and liberal democracy as hostile to their principles because it tolerates alternative lifestyles. Where such zealots are willing to use terrorism or military power to advance their vision, it may not be long before the embryonic institutions of an emergent democracy are trampled underfoot.

Failed attempts to impose democratic values

Though the prospects for establishing liberal democracy in places with problems like these are not promising, many Western governments have been keen to try, believing that democracy is the best solution. Believing that democracy promotes peace, freedom and prosperity, they may want others to enjoy these benefits. They may see democratic institutions, such as free elections and universal franchise, as a way of driving social and political reform. They may even regard democracy as an ideal in itself, the expression of important principles such as human dignity and political equality.

Yet their attempts to export democracy to other countries have enjoyed limited success and have often been quite inept. For example, the Iraq War of 2003 onwards began with the limited purpose of removing an autocratic dictatorship. There seemed to be an assumption that, once this happened, the ideas, principles and institutions of liberal democracy would somehow spring back to life. But that proved over-optimistic. And sadly, the systematic removal of the regime's loyalists left key institutions (police, courts, civil administration) leaderless – creating chaos, destroying trust and making it *more* difficult to introduce democratic reforms.

International institutions

Could international institutions, such as the United Nations, do a better job of moving the world to democracy? There are many reasons to remain sceptical about this idea.

First, international bodies such as the World Bank or International Monetary Fund are often regarded as neo-colonialist – using their wealth to impose their particular concept of government on others. For example, they may deny financial aid to nations that do not match up to their vision of public accountability.

Second, many international agencies are weighted towards the larger or older world powers. China, France, Russia, the UK and the US, for example, have veto power over any substantive United Nations resolution; yet Japan, Germany and India are all economically larger than the UK and France.

Third, many people question whether the United Nations can ever be a credible force for liberal democracy when its own Human Rights Council includes nations such as the Congo and Eritrea, which score badly on international indexes of freedom.

A fourth criticism is that international institutions represent governments, not peoples. Often those governments are despised and hated by their own population, or large sections of it. Yet their delegates purport to speak for the whole country. Bodies composed like this are unlikely to be trusted drivers of democratic reform.

World democracy?

For at least a century, idealists have dreamed of establishing a world democratic government. There are severe problems with this too.

First, democracy is unlikely to work at a global level. How could a population of 7,800 million ever really participate in a global election process? How could we structure a world government that represented everyone fairly – without the big economic powers or big populations taking control? And given the differences in the world's thinking, culture, history, trade links, affiliations and outlook, how could anyone purport to represent 'the world' anyway?

Even modest attempts at supranational government have proved difficult. For example, nearly thirty countries are represented in the Parliament of the European Union. This is popularly elected, but with so many nations and parties involved, and so many different national interests in play, it has very little authority or power. The real decisions are made in unelected bodies of representatives of national governments. Critics complain of 'democratic deficit' but it is hard to see how democracy can be made to work beyond nation states.

Second, the larger that institutions grow, the harder it is to make them transparent and accountable to those they supposedly represent. With world government, the distance (both physical and metaphorical) between the government and the governed, plus the jarring diversity of languages and international viewpoints, are simply too great to make real representation, scrutiny or even communication possible. Electors would be even more alienated from such a body than they are from their own domestic government.

Remember too that countries' legal systems differ. Having developed over centuries, they are deeply rooted, reflecting different historical, cultural, linguistic and social settings. They start from different presumptions and work on different principles. They even encapsulate distinct, opposing views of law and justice. It is optimistic to believe that such differences can be ignored and such diverse systems harmonised. But democracy can only exist on an agreed basis of the rule of law.

A system for small groups?

Democracy works most easily within small groups. In smaller countries, there are more likely to be shared values, strong networks of interpersonal relationships, a sense of mutual belonging, and greater trust. In larger societies where there may be many different groups with different values, and where people do not know each other so closely, trust can be more difficult to achieve.

Yet trust *can* be achieved in larger societies, and democracies built upon it too – even though, as Vincent Ostrom (1997) explains, the process may be difficult and take considerable time. There may also have to be special arrangements to make the democratic institutions work. For example, countries in which there are strong differences, such as a mixture of different ethnicities or languages, may develop federal systems that limit the extent to which decisions can be made centrally: Switzerland and Canada are examples. It may also be significant that the largest democratic countries by land area (for example, Canada, the US, Australia and India) employ federal systems.

Again, there are numerous examples round the world of countries which have created democratic governments in the most unpromising places. Others who seek the benefits of democracy have plenty of options to copy and amend to their own circumstances. It may not be easy, but (for all their complaints about politicians) most people who live in relatively liberal democracies would still argue that it is definitely worth the effort.

13 THE LESSONS OF EXPERIENCE

Do we really want democracy?

'Democracy used to be a bad word', wrote the Canadian political scientist C. B. Macpherson (1966). 'Everybody who was anybody knew that democracy, in its original sense of rule by the people or government in accord with the will of the bulk of the people, would be a bad thing – fatal to individual freedom ... Then, within fifty years, democracy became a good thing'.

Democracy may be a popular idea, but it is more difficult to understand, and practise, than most people think. It rests on a culture of respect for individual rights, the rule of law, toleration, and trusted institutions – all of which may take a long time to evolve. That is why attempts to bring democracy to other cultures (such as post-dictatorial regimes in North Africa, the Middle East and Asia) have often ended in disaster and created only a different kind of tyranny – of majorities, of ideologies, or of religious orthodoxies.

People imagine democracy as some ideal form of 'government of the people, by the people and for the people', as US President Abraham Lincoln (1863) put it in his Gettysburg Address. But modern democracy is no such thing: the people merely choose representatives who then make the decisions. If you are on the losing side, it is hardly a government 'for' you. And who exactly are 'the people'? It took centuries for women to get the vote; and some countries are deeply divided between different ethnic 'peoples'. There is also a wider philosophical question about what right any majority should have to 'govern' the minority in any case.

Democracy may foster useful values such as political equality and inclusion, justice, accountability and social engagement. The English novelist E. M. Forster (1951) gave 'two cheers for democracy', 'one because it admits variety and two because it permits criticism'. But even if democracy is good in itself, that is not enough. It needs to deliver good outcomes too. We can justify democracy only if it *works*.

What justifies democracy?

As the twentieth-century Austrian political economist Joseph Schumpeter (1942) observed, the masses in the middle ages might well have voted for the burning of witches. And even today there are places where majorities believe it perfectly acceptable to persecute minorities they disapprove of.

However, we must not assume that the majority has the unquestioned authority to rule others, or that majority decisions are automatically 'right' and 'just'. Having experienced the alternatives, today's more educated, enlightened and liberal populations have come to the conclusion that majority rule is *not* humanity's value. Things like toleration and respect for the lives of others stand above it.

But if democracy does not exist to give unchecked power to majorities, by what measure can we judge whether it is working? There are many possibilities: whether it really reduces conflict and allows power to be transferred peacefully, for example, or whether the decisions that emerge from it are actually long-sighted, focused and efficient.

What would a sustainable democracy look like?

To work and endure, democracy needs to stay focused on its core purposes – which to the liberal mind means to preserve the rights of individuals, reduce coercion, and to decide those few things (and only those things) that must be decided but can only be decided collectively. It must put rights first and acknowledge them as essential for protecting individuals against coercion, by others or by the state. Without such qualities, democracies are not likely to last for long.

> Democracies have ever been spectacles of turbulence and contention ... and have been in general as short in their lives as they have been violent in their deaths.
> — James Madison (1787), *Federalist No. 10*

Yet there is a minimum set of institutions that might help to give democracy a reasonably long life. There need to be binding rules to curb the power of the voting majority and their representatives. There must be free, fair and competitive elections that offer electors a genuine set of choices. There must be broad protection of civil liberties, a free press, freedom of speech and free association without intimidation by the authorities. There must be no militaries, monarchies or religious orthodoxies with the power to override the choices of the public and legislators.

Today, full adult suffrage is seen as essential, and it would be difficult to construct a modern democracy without it. Yet we need to accept that voters sometimes make disastrous decisions – in 1932, for example, they made the Nazis the largest party in Germany's Reichstag. And even in the most liberal countries, electors do not always vote for what they believe is best for the country, but what is best for themselves. Many voters are also dependent on the state for a living, which inevitably prejudices their electoral choices. Some voters may lack even the competence to make sensible choices. We would not allow incompetent jurists to decide someone's freedom, notes Jason Brennan (2016), so why allow incompetent voters to take the freedom of everyone? But then there is no objective and non-controversial way of settling the competence of electors: we just have to hope that democracy is strong enough to withstand their mistakes.

'There is never a democracy that did not commit suicide', wrote America's second president, John Adams (1814). Yet a democracy is strongest, paradoxically, if people are free to leave it. Voting with your feet sends a more powerful message to the authorities than the mere act of casting a ballot. If government is working to people's benefit, as Jayme Lemke (2016) said, they are more likely stay; if not, and they leave, there may be stronger pressure to reform things. Federal systems may provide the easiest escape, since individuals can move with little difficulty between different provinces with different governmental systems. But today, international migration is a growing option.

Alternative democratic systems

Democracy may have problems, but they are not automatically solved by having 'more' democracy. Direct voting on laws in referendums and ballot initiatives can lead to populist and contradictory results, while deliberative systems and online voting may merely reinforce the flaws that already exist. There are practical issues too – ordinary people do not have the time and interest to spend deliberating policy, which means that policymaking can become captured by those who are fascinated by it, but who do not represent the public. And by making majority decision-making look more legitimate, such 'participation' mechanisms may threaten minorities even more.

But then, how much collective decision-making do we need? Societies have a surprising ability to organise themselves without requiring collective decisions or orders from above. *Spontaneous order*, as the Austrian economist F. A. Hayek (1988) called it, is all around us: in markets, in the way language develops, in online institutions such as Wikipedia and most importantly in the common law that grows naturally through the interaction between individuals. All it takes is a few simple rules of action and morality. Put simply, *don't hurt people and don't take their stuff*, as the American political activist Matt Kibbe (2014) put it in a book of the same title.

On that moral basis, people can set up their own communities – civil society organisations or indeed small government units. Having lots of different administrative units provides people with choice, and with the opportunity to escape from any particular one if they feel they are being ignored or exploited. That of course would be impossible under a 'world government'. Furthermore, the rules that make the spontaneous society function are likely to be simpler and more consensual in small groups. Democracy is a set of human institutions based on agreement and directed at reaching agreement. That requires human contact: democracy does not work in the abstract.

Technology, again, offers us more control over our own lives without needing others to plan our lives for us. IT allows small groups to identify and come together for mutual interest. Who then needs big government? State services and social insurance can be done in new ways more tailored to individuals; commerce and trade can be liberalised as new person-to-person trading systems emerge online.

Indeed, the argument that people cannot govern themselves (once used to deny votes to women and slaves) looks increasingly hollow. People are innovative. Today, they can and do organise themselves – and their taxis, holiday accommodation, deliveries, utilities and more – efficiently and in sophisticated ways online, without the whole society needing to make collective decisions for everyone.

Democracy isn't everything

Enthusiasts for democracy generally want to see more of it – spreading it more widely to other countries and deepening collective decision-making in their own. They should instead accept that majority decision-making is imperfect, and that the decisions of 'the people' (however we define them) are not automatically legitimate – as with witch-burning.

Democracy, on the contrary, is only one element of good government, along with the rule of law, individual rights, toleration, free speech and much else. To work well, democracy has to be limited in its scope to its essential tasks, leaving a secure private sphere in which individuals can act as they choose. And it has to be limited in its actions, in ways that prevent force and power being abused and used against, not for, the population. That might require constitutional restraints, the balance of powers, and super-majorities for some decisions. But this *liberal democracy* also requires a deeper culture and understanding.

Democracy is demanding. It requires human cooperation on a large scale. It requires self-control, particularly by those in the majority or in positions of authority. It requires us to forgo personal advantage and immediate satisfaction for something more long term. It requires us to accept our mistakes and learn from them willingly and honestly. It is not an off-the-shelf package because it must be tailored to whatever historical and cultural environment it occupies. It requires the general acceptance of all sorts of rules, both the overarching world view that makes it work and the smaller conventions (almost like 'manners') that make it work well. It requires an open society – a society of a manageable and human size, but one willing to interact with other open societies worldwide.

As for our politicians, they could aim to promote the self-organisation of citizens, not try to organise citizens themselves. And there is a case for political intervention to be minimised: society is too complex for any central authorities to plan, manage or even understand.

Personal freedom requires no justification: you suffer the consequences of anything you do. Democracy, however, does require justification, because *others* suffer the consequences of what you do.

Should we hail democracy as justified? It is still an experiment in progress. Democracy is more closely associated with liberal values such as the respect for individual and human rights, and with the freedom to go out and prosper, than other systems. Once established, it has proved surprisingly stable and enduring. And democratic institutions, even if imperfect, provide a forum in which those who support liberal values can argue their case and explain the practical and moral benefits of genuine liberal democracy.

14 QUOTATIONS ABOUT DEMOCRACY

The tyranny of the majority

Unlimited democracy is, just like oligarchy, a tyranny spread over a large number of people.

> — Aristotle (*c.* 350 BC), *Politics*

Democracy is not freedom. Democracy is two wolves and a lamb voting on what to have for lunch. Freedom comes from the recognition of certain rights which may not be taken, not even by a 99% vote.

> — Marvin Simkin (1992),
> 'Individual Rights', *Los Angeles Times*

Power corrupts

As soon as people have power they go crooked and sometimes dotty as well, because the possession of power lifts them into a region where normal honesty never pays.

> — E. M. Forster (1951), *Two Cheers for Democracy*

All governments suffer a recurring problem: *Power attracts pathological personalities.* It is not that power corrupts but that it is magnetic to the corruptible.

> — Frank Herbert (1965), *Dune*

I am inclined to think that rulers have rarely been above the average, either morally or intellectually, and often below it. And I think that it is reasonable to adopt, in politics, the principle of preparing for the worst ...

— Karl Popper (1945), *The Open Society and Its Enemies*

The culture of democracy

If liberty and equality, as is thought by some are chiefly to be found in democracy, they will be best attained when all persons alike share in the government to the utmost.

— Aristotle (*c.* 350 BC), *Politics*

By sacrificing the individual to the State, the rulers of the Roman world undermined the real virtues which sustained it. They turned active and self-respecting citizens into inert and selfish ones.

— Sir Arthur Bryant (1984), *Set in a Silver Sea: A History of Britain and the British People*

No representative should blindly follow the opinions of party, when in direct opposition to your own clear ideas; a degree of servitude that no worthy man could bear the thought of submitting to.

— Edmund Burke (1741), *The Gentleman's and London Magazine*

The world must be made safe for democracy. Its peace must be planted upon the tested foundations of political liberty.

— Woodrow Wilson (1917), *Address to Congress on War*

FURTHER READING

Explanations and overviews

Beetham, D. (2005) *Democracy: A Beginner's Guide.* London: Oneworld Publications. A straightforward introduction, spelling out the principles and institutions needed to make democracy work and comparing how it actually evolves in reality. The book explains the problems of emergent democracies, the disillusionment with politics more generally, and participative alternatives.

Butler, E. (2012) *Public Choice: A Primer.* London: Institute of Economic Affairs. Straightforward guide to the role of self-interest among voters, pressure groups, politicians and officials, and how this calls the efficiency and objectivity of democratic decisions into question.

Butler, E. (2013) *Foundations of a Free Society.* London: Institute of Economic Affairs. Simple exposition of the principles that underpin social and economic freedom and liberal democracy, such as toleration, justice, property rights and civic equality.

Crick, B. (2003) *Democracy: A Very Short Introduction.* Oxford University Press. Traces the history of democracy from Ancient Greece before explaining issues such as populism, the institutions of good government, and citizenship.

Cartledge, P. (2018) *Democracy: A Life.* Oxford University Press. Large history tracing the roots of democracy from Ancient Greece through the Roman Republic, Renaissance systems, the American Constitution to the liberal democracies of today – and how each system has dealt with the issue of rights versus majorities.

Weale, A. (2007) *Democracy*. London: Palgrave. Slightly theoretical and philosophical but raises some good questions about the nature of democracy, the challenges to it, and how it can only be judged with respect to our deeper values.

Challenges and critiques

Achen, C. and Bartels, L. (2017) *Democracy for Realists*. Princeton University Press. Good overview of the problems of voter ignorance, tribalism and short-termism. The authors reject ballot initiatives and other participative solutions in favour of having regular and frequent elections to prevent the accumulation of power.

Brennan, J. (2016) *Against Democracy*. Princeton University Press. A philosopher points out the systematic biases of voters, arguing that they cannot be 'educated' out of these by participative systems, and that they are only made worse by them. He argues that democracy trivialises complex choices, rests on force, allows individuals to dominate others and so makes strangers into enemies.

Caplan, B. (2007) *The Myth of the Rational Voter*. Princeton University Press. The classic explanation of how voters have systematic biases – specifically, anti-market, anti-foreign, make-work and pessimistic biases – that distort democratic outcomes and explain why democracy fails.

Karsten, F. and Beckman, K. (2012) *Beyond Democracy*. Scotts Valley, CA: CreateSpace. Logical and straightforward critique from a libertarian perspective, explaining that democracy is a collectivist idea now in crisis. The authors list the myths – of popular rule, fairness, freedom, tolerance, etc. – that are attributed to democracy and highlight its problems – including bureaucracy, welfarism and short-termism. They advocate a new idea of smaller governments with simple basic laws.

Ostrom, V. (1997) *The Meaning of Democracy and Vulnerability of Democracies.* University of Michigan Press. Exploration of the social and cultural conditions needed for a democratic system to flourish, and of the difficulty of preserving individual freedoms and civil society in the face of powerful 'democratic' governments. Also explores the difficulties of building democratic societies in various continents, and particularly in countries emerging from communism.

Smith, C. and Miers, T. (2011) *Democracy and the Fall of the West.* Exeter: Imprint Academic. This short book argues that democracy is creating a new tyranny that undermines the liberal values on which it is built – such as the rule of law, toleration, property rights, free markets, civil society and social freedom. Politicians see democracy as a useful source of power for their own projects, leading to an overbearing state.

Stoker, G. (2007) *Why Politics Matters: Making Democracy Work.* New York: Palgrave Macmillan. Points out that politics is an inevitable part of democracy because collective decisions are so important to everyone. But politics has become a 'profession' that leaves the public alienated – and made cynical by the media's coverage of it. Calls for greater accountability, party spending caps, citizen recall and more localism.

Other references

Acemoglu, D. and Robinson, J. (2006) *Economic Origins of Dictatorship and Democracy.* Cambridge University Press.

Acemoglu, D. and Robinson, J. (2012) *Why Nations Fail.* New York: Crown Publishing Group.

Adams, J. (1814) Letter to John Taylor (XVIII). Washington, DC: National Archives (https://founders.archives.gov/documents/Adams/99-02-02-6371).

Alves, A. and Meadowcroft, J. (2014) Hayek's slippery slope, the stability of the mixed economy and the dynamics of rent seeking. *Political Studies* 62(4): 843–61.

Aristotle (350 BC) *Politics.*

Attlee, C. (1957) Speech at Oxford, 14 June.

Brennan, G. and Buchanan, J. M. (1980) *The Power to Tax. Analytic Foundations of a Fiscal Constitution.* Cambridge University Press.

Burke, E. (1774) Speech to the electors of Bristol (https://www.econlib.org/book-chapters/chapter-vol-4-miscellaneous-writings-speech-to-the-electors-of-bristol/).

Burke, E. (1790) *Reflections on the Revolution in France.* London: James Dodsley.

Butler, E. (2015a) *Classical Liberalism: A Primer.* London: Institute of Economic Affairs.

Butler, E. (2015b) *Magna Carta: A Primer.* London: Adam Smith Institute.

Economist Intelligence Unit (2019) Democracy Index 2019 (http://www.eiu.com/topic/democracy-index).

Forster, E. M. (1951) *Two Cheers for Democracy.* New York: Harcourt, Brace and Company.

Fukuyama, F. (1992) *The End of History and the Last Man*. New York: Free Press.

Hayek, F. A. (1944) *The Road to Serfdom*. London: Routledge.

Hayek, F. A. (1979) *Law, Legislation and Liberty*, Volume 1. London: Routledge.

Hayek, F. A. (1988) *The Fatal Conceit: The Errors of Socialism*. London: Routledge.

Hobbes, T. (1651) *Leviathan*. London: Andrew Crooke.

Hume, D. (1758) *Essays, Moral, Political and Literary*. Edinburgh: Alexander Kincaid.

Kennedy, A. (1999) *Frontline* interview: Justice for Sale. Public Broadcasting System.

Kibbe, M. (2014) *Don't Hurt People and Don't Take Their Stuff*. New York: Harper Collins.

Lawson, R., Murphy, R. and Powell, B. (2020) The determinants of economic freedom: a survey. *Contemporary Economic Policy* 38(4): 622–42.

Lemke, J. S. (2016) Interjurisdictional competition and the Married Women's Property Acts. *Public Choice* 166(3): 291–313.

Lincoln, A. (1863) Gettysburg Address (http://www.ourdocuments.gov/doc.php?doc=36&page=transcript).

Locke, J. (1689) Second treatise of government. In *Two Treatises of Government*. London: Awnsham Churchill.

Luxemburg, R. (1899) *Social Reform or Revolution?* (https://www.marxists.org/archive/luxemburg/1900/reform-revolution/).

Machiavelli, N. (1513) *The Prince*. Rome: Antonio Blado d'Asola.

Macpherson, C. B. (1966) *The Real World of Democracy*. Oxford: Clarendon Press.

Matsusaka, J. G. (2004) *For the Many or the Few: The Initiative, Public Policy and American Democracy*. Chicago University Press.

Mencken, H. L. (1956) *Minority Report*. Baltimore: Johns Hopkins University Press.

Mesquita, B. B. De, Smith, A., Siverson, R. M., Morrow, J. D. (2003) *The Logic of Political Survival*. Cambridge, MA: MIT Press.

Mill, J. S. (1861) *Considerations on Representative Government*. London: Parker, Son, and Bourn

Montesquieu, C.-L. (1748) *The Spirit of the Laws* (https://oll.lib ertyfund.org/title/montesquieu-complete-works-vol-1-the -spirit-of-laws).

Murphy, R. (2018) Governance and the dimensions of autocracy. *Constitutional Political Economy* 30: 131–48.

Orwell, G. (1946) Politics and the English language. *Horizon* 13(76): 252–65.

Pericles of Athens (*c.* 431 BC) Funeral Oration. In *The History of the Peloponnesian War*.

Popper, K. R. (1945) *The Open Society and Its Enemies*. London: Routledge.

Ridley, M. (2020) *How Innovation Works*. London: Fourth Estate.

Robespierre, M. (1794) *Report on the Principles of Public Morality*. Philadelphia: Benjamin Franklin Bache.

Schumpeter, J. (1942) *Capitalism, Socialism and Democracy*. New York: Harper & Brothers.

Tocqueville, A. de (1835) *Democracy in America*. London: Saunders and Otley.

Transparency International (2019) *Corruption Perceptions Index*. Berlin: Transparency International.

Vidal, G. (1987) *Armageddon*. London: Grafton.

KEY TERMS

Autocracy

From the Greek *autos* (self) and *kratos* (power). A form of government in which a single person (*autocrat*) exercises control without being subject to any legal or electoral restraint.

Ballot initiative

A proposal, initiated by a group of voters, to adopt a policy, force a vote in the legislature, or call a referendum.

Constitution

A body of convention, law and precedent that specifies how government is to be structured and operate, and the limits to the power of those involved.

Constitutional government

Any form of government in which power is defined and limited by basic laws, conventions or written ('codified') constitutions. They include *constitutional monarchy* in which the position of head of state is inherited, *constitutional democracy* in which the qualifying citizens can choose and hold accountable those in power, and *constitutional oligarchy* where authority is wielded by a group.

Democracy

From the Greek *demos* (people) and *kratos* (power). In Ancient Greece, the form of government in which the eligible citizens of a city state would meet together to debate and decide laws and policies. Today, any form of government in which eligible citizens choose representatives who debate and decide laws and policies.

Dictator

From the Latin *dicto* (dictate). A ruler with absolute power over a country, typically one who has obtained control by force.

Liberal democracy

A form of democracy which gives priority to individual rights and freedoms over majority rule. Liberal democracy is characterised by free and fair elections, the separation of powers, toleration and the rule of law.

Oligarchy

From the Greek *olígos* (few) and *arkho* (rule). A form of government controlled by a small group such as a family or military junta.

Recall

A procedure by which local electors can eject their representative from office outside the normal election cycle.

Referendum

A vote of the whole electorate on some issue, usually initiated by the government. The result may be binding on the legislature and executive, or merely advisory.

Republic

From the Latin *res publica* (thing of the people). A form of government in which power is not inherited but comes through election by the public or appointment by elected representatives and sometimes by oligarchs or an autocrat. Power in republics is usually limited by agreed conventions or a written constitution. The head of state is usually a president.

Separation of powers

The system that seeks to limit the accumulation of power by separating government functions into different branches such as the executive, the legislature and the judiciary. Commonly, legislative power is further divided between two different houses or chambers of the legislature.

ABOUT THE IEA

The Institute is a research and educational charity (No. CC 235 351), limited by guarantee. Its mission is to improve understanding of the fundamental institutions of a free society by analysing and expounding the role of markets in solving economic and social problems.

The IEA achieves its mission by:

- a high-quality publishing programme
- conferences, seminars, lectures and other events
- outreach to school and college students
- brokering media introductions and appearances

The IEA, which was established in 1955 by the late Sir Antony Fisher, is an educational charity, not a political organisation. It is independent of any political party or group and does not carry on activities intended to affect support for any political party or candidate in any election or referendum, or at any other time. It is financed by sales of publications, conference fees and voluntary donations.

In addition to its main series of publications, the IEA also publishes (jointly with the University of Buckingham), *Economic Affairs*.

The IEA is aided in its work by a distinguished international Academic Advisory Council and an eminent panel of Honorary Fellows. Together with other academics, they review prospective IEA publications, their comments being passed on anonymously to authors. All IEA papers are therefore subject to the same rigorous independent refereeing process as used by leading academic journals.

IEA publications enjoy widespread classroom use and course adoptions in schools and universities. They are also sold throughout the world and often translated/reprinted.

Since 1974 the IEA has helped to create a worldwide network of 100 similar institutions in over 70 countries. They are all independent but share the IEA's mission.

Views expressed in the IEA's publications are those of the authors, not those of the Institute (which has no corporate view), its Managing Trustees, Academic Advisory Council members or senior staff.

Members of the Institute's Academic Advisory Council, Honorary Fellows, Trustees and Staff are listed on the following page.

The Institute gratefully acknowledges financial support for its publications programme and other work from a generous benefaction by the late Professor Ronald Coase.

Other books recently published by the IEA include:

In Focus: The Case for Privatising the BBC
Edited by Philip Booth
Hobart Paperback 182; ISBN 978-0-255-36725-7; £12.50

Islamic Foundations of a Free Society
Edited by Nouh El Harmouzi and Linda Whetstone
Hobart Paperback 183; ISBN 978-0-255-36728-8; £12.50

The Economics of International Development: Foreign Aid versus Freedom for the World's Poor
William Easterly
Readings in Political Economy 6; ISBN 978-0-255-36731-8; £7.50

Taxation, Government Spending and Economic Growth
Edited by Philip Booth
Hobart Paperback 184; ISBN 978-0-255-36734-9; £15.00

Universal Healthcare without the NHS: Towards a Patient-Centred Health System
Kristian Niemietz
Hobart Paperback 185; ISBN 978-0-255-36737-0; £10.00

Sea Change: How Markets and Property Rights Could Transform the Fishing Industry
Edited by Richard Wellings
Readings in Political Economy 7; ISBN 978-0-255-36740-0; £10.00

Working to Rule: The Damaging Economics of UK Employment Regulation
J. R. Shackleton
Hobart Paperback 186; ISBN 978-0-255-36743-1; £15.00

Education, War and Peace: The Surprising Success of Private Schools in War-Torn Countries
James Tooley and David Longfield
ISBN 978-0-255-36746-2; £10.00

Killjoys: A Critique of Paternalism
Christopher Snowdon
ISBN 978-0-255-36749-3; £12.50

Financial Stability without Central Banks
George Selgin, Kevin Dowd and Mathieu Bédard
ISBN 978-0-255-36752-3; £10.00

Against the Grain: Insights from an Economic Contrarian
Paul Ormerod
ISBN 978-0-255-36755-4; £15.00

Ayn Rand: An Introduction
Eamonn Butler
ISBN 978-0-255-36764-6; £12.50

Capitalism: An Introduction
Eamonn Butler
ISBN 978-0-255-36758-5; £12.50

Opting Out: Conscience and Cooperation in a Pluralistic Society
David S. Oderberg
ISBN 978-0-255-36761-5; £12.50

Getting the Measure of Money: A Critical Assessment of UK Monetary Indicators
Anthony J. Evans
ISBN 978-0-255-36767-7; £12.50

Socialism: The Failed Idea That Never Dies
Kristian Niemietz
ISBN 978-0-255-36770-7; £17.50

Top Dogs and Fat Cats: The Debate on High Pay
Edited by J. R. Shackleton
ISBN 978-0-255-36773-8; £15.00

School Choice around the World … And the Lessons We Can Learn
Edited by Pauline Dixon and Steve Humble
ISBN 978-0-255-36779-0; £15.00

School of Thought: 101 Great Liberal Thinkers
Eamonn Butler
ISBN 978-0-255-36776-9; £12.50

Raising the Roof: How to Solve the United Kingdom's Housing Crisis
Edited by Jacob Rees-Mogg and Radomir Tylecote
ISBN 978-0-255-36782-0; £12.50

How Many Light Bulbs Does It Take to Change the World?
Matt Ridley and Stephen Davies
ISBN 978-0-255-36785-1; £10.00

The Henry Fords of Healthcare: …Lessons the West Can Learn from the East
Nima Sanandaji
ISBN 978-0-255-36788-2; £10.00

An Introduction to Entrepreneurship
Eamonn Butler
ISBN 978-0-255-36794-3; £12.50

Other IEA publications

Comprehensive information on other publications and the wider work of the IEA can be found at www.iea.org.uk. To order any publication please see below.

Personal customers

Orders from personal customers should be directed to the IEA:

Clare Rusbridge
IEA
2 Lord North Street
FREEPOST LON10168
London SW1P 3YZ
Tel: 020 7799 8911, Fax: 020 7799 2137
Email: sales@iea.org.uk

Trade customers

All orders from the book trade should be directed to the IEA's distributor:

NBN International (IEA Orders)
Orders Dept.
NBN International
10 Thornbury Road
Plymouth PL6 7PP
Tel: 01752 202301, Fax: 01752 202333
Email: orders@nbninternational.com

IEA subscriptions

The IEA also offers a subscription service to its publications. For a single annual payment (currently £42.00 in the UK), subscribers receive every monograph the IEA publishes. For more information please contact:

Clare Rusbridge
Subscriptions
IEA
2 Lord North Street
FREEPOST LON10168
London SW1P 3YZ
Tel: 020 7799 8911, Fax: 020 7799 2137
Email: crusbridge@iea.org.uk